William Hardman

A Trip to America

William Hardman

A Trip to America

ISBN/EAN: 9783337145354

Printed in Europe, USA, Canada, Australia, Japan

Cover: Foto ©Andreas Hilbeck / pixelio.de

More available books at **www.hansebooks.com**

A

TRIP TO AMERICA.

BY

WILLIAM HARDMAN.

WITH MAP.

LONDON:
T. VICKERS WOOD, CHURTON STREET,
BELGRAVE ROAD, S.W.

1884.

TO ALL

OUR AMERICAN FRIENDS,

WHOSE KINDNESS WE CAN NEVER FORGET,

BUT MORE ESPECIALLY TO OUR

GENIAL HOST,

RUFUS HATCH,

MORE FAMILIARLY KNOWN AS

" UNCLE RUFUS,"

TO WHOSE UNBOUNDED HOSPITALITY,

MY WIFE AND MYSELF,

ARE INDEBTED FOR ONE OF THE GREATEST

ENJOYMENTS OF OUR LIVES.

CONTENTS.

CHAP.		PAGE.
I.	ACROSS THE ATLANTIC	1
II.	NEW YORK AND ITS WAYS	10
III.	THE "CONFIDENCE MEN" OF NEW YORK	17
IV.	NEW YORK AND ITS FOOD	26
V.	SOME PECULIARITIES OF NEW YORK	34
VI.	NEW YORK THEATRES AND PRISONS	44
VII.	HOSPITALS AND ASYLUMS	53
VIII.	THE IMMIGRANTS AT CASTLE GARDEN	60
IX.	NEW YORK—HELL GATE AND THE HUDSON	67
X.	A RAILWAY JOURNEY—NIAGARA	73
XI.	CHICAGO	82
XII.	CHICAGO: STOCK YARDS; PULLMAN; CHURCHES	92
XIII.	THE NORTHERN PACIFIC RAILROAD—ST. PAUL—MINNEAPOLIS	101
XIV.	FARGO	112
XV.	ACROSS THE PRAIRIE—THE GROS VENTRES	124
XVI.	LITTLE MISSOURI TO THE WONDERLAND	133
XVII.	THE GATE OF THE MOUNTAINS	140
XVIII.	THE MAMMOTH HOT SPRINGS	147
XIX.	THE GEYSER BASINS	157
XX.	SITTING BULL AT BISMARCK	176
XXI.	BACK TO NEW YORK—WASHINGTON	188
XXII.	WASHINGTON—PHILADELPHIA	197

INTRODUCTORY.

I AM not fond of Tables of "Errata," but I am most anxious to correct a few errors into which I have inadvertently fallen, and which have been pointed out to me too late for amendment in the body of the work.

The Hon. Roscoe Conkling has never been Attorney-General of the United States. He is an ex-Senator, and has been offered, but declined, the position of Judge of the Supreme Court.

Mr. E. A. Quintard, our genial companion, is a very popular member of the Union League Club, but is not the President of the Club. He is President of one of the largest Saving Banks in New York.

With regard to my remarks on the East River Bridge, an American friend writes:—
"The opposition to opening the Bridge on the Queen's Birthday, originated among, and was sustained by, Irish Dynamite Clubs and their sympathisers. I never heard a real native American object to it, and when, at last, some of the Irish in a 'League' or 'Council' meeting, openly advocated violence and the use of dynamite against the Bridge structure, unless the Trustees made a change in the time of opening the Bridge, the better sentiment—the American sentiment—crystallized in a day. Instantly there were universal demands that the Trustees should adhere to the day fixed, and the fidelity of the troops who were to take part in the parade and ceremony, was referred to as sufficient to sustain the Trustees, if necessary to do so, by force."

A TRIP TO AMERICA.

CHAPTER I.

ACROSS THE ATLANTIC.

THE number of English visitors to the United States and Canada is rapidly increasing. During the past year various causes have been at work to encourage this sort of emigration. Every Englishman who can spare the time and the money—the latter being a very important factor in the enterprise—should visit the great English-speaking nation on the other side of the Atlantic. He cannot fail to return with his mind enlarged, his sympathies quickened, and his Old World ideas of hospitality greatly extended. He will feel pride in the enterprise and advance of the Anglo-Saxon race; but he will not escape a sense of sadness when he realises what has been lost to England by the folly and mismanagement of its rulers a century ago. However, that is a lesson which it is well to learn, especially in these days, when so little trouble is taken to keep on pleasant terms with colonial dependencies.

The dread of the long voyage of over 3,000 miles deters many people, especially ladies; but these terrors are all in anticipation, rarely, if ever, in fact. Messrs. Ismay, Imrie & Co., the spirited owners of the White Star Line of Steamships, have revolutionised not only the time taken by the voyage, but have in every way so added to the comforts and convenience of their passengers, that the end of even only a tolerable passage is viewed with regret. I went out in the *Adriatic* and returned in the *Britannic*, two of the finest ships in their fleet, and I shall ever recollect with pleasure and gratitude the kindness of the captains and officers of both vessels.

The *Adriatic* carried about 400 steerage passengers, chiefly English, Irish, German, and Scandinavian. There were about 100 saloon passengers, and the crew numbered another 100, making 600 souls in all. The steerage passengers pay 26 dollars each (about £5), for which they have a bunk and their food, but must find their own bedding and utensils. It is impossible not to feel interested in these emigrants. Among them were married couples with young children, the parents, especially the mother, with grave and anxious faces looking forward into the future. There were men without encumbrance, who smoked and chatted cheerily. One of these asked me if I knew of any work for him in New York, when an Irish emigrant, overhearing our conversation, exclaimed, "Oh, the divil take the work! It's not that I want, it's the money."

There were also among these poor travellers not a few old people, especially old women, who had been sent for by their children to share their happier lot in their new home. And there were some Norwegian peasant girls in quaint dresses, much plaited, and very short in the waist. Before landing at New York all the emigrants had to submit to a very strict examination by the doctors belonging to the immigrant department. I was informed that, whether they have undergone the operation previously or not, they must be vaccinated before they are permitted to land, and if the authorities in America say that any particular act must be done, you may rely upon their orders being carried out.

On Saturday afternoon the steerage passengers had a ball, to .the great amusement of us on the saloon deck. Very merry they were until sunset, when, according to inexorable rule, the men were relegated to one end of the ship, and the women to the other.

When Sunday came, one or two well-meaning enthusiasts among our party, anxious for the welfare of the emigrants, tried in the afternoon to get up a sort of informal prayer meeting. But the wind got up at the same time, and the rain came down in torrents, so that the whole affair was a *fiasco*. An increasing greenish pallor rapidly spread over the faces of both speakers and hearers, and the meeting quietly melted away. The purser read prayers in the saloon, and a very impressive scene it was. Our ship by that time had become our little world. We were almost exactly half way. Fifteen hundred miles of ocean separated us from land on either side. I think all our hearts must have thrilled with unaccustomed feeling as we

joined in that beautiful hymn for those at sea—
"Eternal Father, strong to save;"
and I am sure the collection, on behalf of the institution at Liverpool for the widows and orphans of sailors of all nations, was not diminished by this feeling.

Life on board the *Adriatic* was relieved of its monotony by the active interest taken by the purser (Mr. Russell) and the doctor (Mr. Murray) in getting up games on deck, in which the English were always ready to join. A few infatuated persons, chiefly, I believe, Americans, played for considerable stakes at "poker" incessantly in the smoking room from morning to night, but they were not held in high esteem. Amongst other games on deck, Messrs. Russell and Murray organised cricket, which afforded infinite amusement, and no little bodily exercise. The carpenter was called to our aid, and soon constructed the requisite implements. The stumps, which, of course, could not be driven into the deck, had to stand on a flat board. To them the bails were attached by a string six inches in length. The ends of the bats were padded with leather to prevent injury to the deck, which is sacred in a sailor's eyes. But the ball was the most curious arrangement. I believe the carpenter had made that as well as the bats and stumps. It was very soft for a cricket ball, and not very perfect in shape, but it sufficed. Externally it was of canvas, to which was attached a long piece of cord about 20 yards in length, the other end of the cord being tied to a stanchion. This cord was always doing unexpected things. It got under the feet of the bowler, and checked the ball in its mad career; it tied itself in knots; it got wet and twisted. But, no matter, whatever it did only added to the fun. So, with the aid of shuffle-board, deck quoits, cricket, reading and chatting, the monotony of the Atlantic Ocean was relieved. We were soon off the tail of the Great Bank of Newfoundland and approaching the American coast. The fogs were rather troublesome, not only because they delayed us, but because they called into use that fearful instrument of torture, the fog-horn, which for one entire night, at half-minute intervals, bellowed and trumpeted like a herd of elephants.

The first "touch," so to speak, of the other

side is the pilot, who came on board more than 300 miles from New York. The excitement as the time approaches for the arrival of this functionary is very amusing. There is a sweepstake as to his number, which is seen in gigantic figures on the sail of his boat. Then bets are freely made as to which foot he will place on board first; whether he will be light or dark, married or single, any children, how many more sons than daughters, or the reverse, and so on. The lady passenger who first sees his sail is entitled by a singular custom to a bottle of whiskey, which was duly sent to the cabin of the fortunate winner, after which I can only add that nothing more was heard of it. Sometimes the pilot comes on board 500, and even 600, miles from New York. This is the result of the rivalry and competition between them, for the pay is very handsome.

Our last night at sea was enlivened by a mild dose of the fog horn, but at sunrise the mist cleared away and we could distinguish the low sandy shore of Long Island on our right. The gigantic hotel, with its 700 beds, on Rockaway Beach loomed through the hot morning haze. The English passengers gazed with interest as the coast gradually passed in review before them, while our American friends evidently enjoyed the pleasure of pointing out the different places and explaining everything that was needed. The Navesink Highlands, on our left, stood out in bold relief, and soon we approached Sandy Hook, familiar to most of us by name, and knew that we were only some twenty miles from New York. Sandy Hook is the extreme northern point of the New Jersey coast, and, as its name almost implies, is a strip of sandy beach projecting into the water. Staten Island, Coney Island, Brooklyn Bridge, Jersey City, were duly introduced to us by our friends as we steamed by. The strange ferry boats, the uncanny-looking steamtugs, the steam elevators plying for hire to remove grain from canal boat to ship, and all the novel objects on the Hudson River interested us vastly, while the fine harbour of New York excited our warm admiration. We called it picturesque, to which one of our American friends replied, "Yes; it is an *elegant* harbour," thus giving us an early experience of their singular misuse of this adjective, which is applied indiscriminately to a sunset, a mountain, or a piece of beef, but never to a lady.

The *Adriatic* was, with the assistance of an active, fussy little steamtug, backed into one of the numerous little docks which disfigure the water front of the city, and are quite unworthy of the harbour and its vast traffic. The Custom House officers were active and inquisitive in their examination of luggage beyond the officers of any *douane* on the European Continent. The English passengers escaped easily, but the gigantic Saratoga trunks of the Americans were ransacked to the very bottom, especially if their owners were, as was the case in several instances, in the habit of crossing the Atlantic frequently. The difference in the price of articles of clothing, especially for ladies, in London or Paris, and New York, is so great as to go far towards recouping the travellers the expense of the journey.

CHAPTER II.

NEW YORK AND ITS WAYS.

The first thing that strikes the traveller on his arrival in New York is the entire absence of cabs, as we understand them. There are carriages, usually drawn by two horses, for hire. They are similar to the broughams hired from a London livery stable. With the drivers of these vehicles, it is necessary before entering the carriage to have a distinct understanding as to the fare to be paid, for the New York hack driver is never content to accept the legal fare—for there is nominally a legal fare—until he is satisfied he will get no more.

In a conversation with the Hon. Roscoe Conkling, one of the most distinguished Senators of the United States, I mentioned the unsatisfactory nature of the cab accommodation in New York. He entirely endorsed my view, and related to me an incident which occurred to himself. He had crossed from Hoboken by one of the ferry boats to New York, and overheard a lady, with children and luggage, make a bargain with a hack driver to convey her and her belongings to a certain hotel for two dollars. By chance, Mr. Conkling was going to the same hotel, and arrived there just in time to hear the driver, in loud tones, demanding from the unhappy lady three times the fare he had agreed to take. To use Mr. Conkling's own expression, he "went for" the hack driver, with the result that justice was done. The driver might safely bully an unprotected female, but the Attorney-General of the United States was not a person to be hauled before the mayor under such circumstances. Besides, he is considerably over six feet in height, with physique in proportion.

Having made your bargain and entered your carriage, the next thing that strikes you is the exceeding badness of the pavement. We had scarcely jolted 300 yards over rough stone blocks before we were nearly turned over at the corner of a street. The wretched paving of the city may be due to two causes. One is that locomotion is mainly carried on by tramway cars and elevated railroads, and the other, that the money raised by the authorities for this and other purposes does not always find its way into the channel for which it was intended. However, strong efforts are being made to improve the pavements, and I heard a rumour that hansom cabs were soon to be established under the auspices of a wealthy company.

Of course you will have had it dinned into your ears *ad nauseam* that the baggage arrangements in the United States are so superior to ours. " What do you think of our system of checks?" you are asked, "Is it not perfect? You have nothing like it in your country." You admit that it has its merits, but you are not quite unacquainted with it. It is very useful for large packages, whose delivery, if delayed for many hours, is not a matter of supreme importance. But in my case, when all I had in the (new) world was contained in my limited amount of luggage, it was distinctly inconvenient to wait five hours. I tried to be resigned, but I could not help thinking that, had I been landed at a London wharf or railway station, I should have been able to call a "growler" and transport myself and all my belongings to my hotel at the same time.

In Broadway and the principal thoroughfares, the view is obstructed and the general effect of the street and its architecture entirely spoiled, by the forest of lofty telegraph-poles, with their multitudes of cross-bars supporting the wires. It is difficult to understand how such a disfigurement of their city could ever have been tolerated by the New Yorkers. They make much more use of telegraph and telephone than we do. On June 1st, 1877, there were but 200 telephones in use in the United States; at the present time there are 150,000. The telephone is worked over thousands of miles, and the blows of the hammer which drove the last spike of the Northern Pacific Railway, in the territory of Montana, were heard at New York, 3,000 miles away. In fact, electricity in its various uses is more general than with us. The electric light, instead of being the exception, is almost the rule, and you meet with it as you journey onwards at every place of any importance.

If the telegraph poles are a disfigurement, the elevated railways are more so. On iron piers and girders, on the level with the first-floor windows, run these trains at three-minute intervals during the day. They form a species of arcade above the tracks of the horse railroads, and however convenient they may be to the general public, they have done great injury to individuals, whose wishes were never consulted, by depreciating the value of property in the streets through which they pass. Efforts are now being strenuously made in the courts to recover compensation, and no doubt so just and reasonable a claim must in the end be admitted.

The fare on all the lines, regardless of distance, is 10 cents, except between 5.30 and 8.30 a.m., and 4.30 and 7.30 p.m., when it is 5 cents. Smoking is not permitted either in the carriages (to be more correct I should call them cars) or in the stations. Passengers being admitted at the ends of the cars, instead of at the sides as in England, and there being no compartments, the seats running down each side from end to end, with a passage in the middle, there is none of that slamming of doors which is so great a nuisance on our Metropolitan Underground line.

The Roman Catholic population of the state of New York exceeds in numbers the whole of the other religious denominations put together, and New York City alone contains no less than fifty-seven Catholic Churches. The Cathedral of St. Patrick, in Fifth Avenue, although unfinished, is a noble building of white marble, majestic in its simplicity. It was projected by one, whom my wife and myself, notwithstanding that we differed from him in creed, were proud to call our friend,— I mean Archbishop Hughes—about 1850, but the corner stone was not laid until 1858. Its architecture is of the same period as the nave of Westminster Abbey.

The Church of St. Francis Xavier, in Sixteenth Street, which is served by the Jesuit fathers of the adjoining College, is a magnificent example of the Renaissance style, and was crowded on the Sunday after our arrival by a congregation of about four thousand persons, eager to listen to the first sermon preached by Monsignor Capel in America. It was the Feast of St. Ignatius Loyola, and the Monsignor, although he was obviously nervous, delivered a very powerful discourse, which was mainly a panegyric on Loyola's character and work. Without great oratorical effort he held the attention of his hearers by his clear resonant voice and sincere manner. An Irishman who gave me a seat in his pew was greatly interested when I told him the Monsignor was a friend of mine, and asked me numerous questions about him. He seemed disappointed when I explained that Capel was not an Irishman, and he could scarcely believe that any Englishman could be a Catholic! Before the sermon my neighbour opined that Capel could not compare with the much beloved Father Tom Burke, but afterwards he was rather shaken in his opinion.

CHAPTER III.

The "Confidence Men" of New York.

Travellers in New York, especially if they bear in their appearance obvious signs of being strangers, will find themselves the objects of much attention from certain persons whom they will inevitably meet in Broadway, Fifth Avenue, or in the vicinity of the wharves. They will be warmly greeted as old friends by individuals they have never seen in their lives. These are the "confidence" men, who literally swarm near the landing-stages.

Walking one day from Broadway to the landing-stage of the White Star Line, I was accosted by no less than four of these rascals in succession. One of them, by getting in my way on the crowded *trottoir*, succeeded in engaging me in conversation.

Offering his hand, he said cheerfully, "How do you do, sir?"

I stared silently at him. He went on—

"You have forgotten me, I daresay."

"No," I replied, "I don't think I have"—he was about to interrupt me cheerily, when I continued—"because I feel sure I never saw you in my life before."

This rather staggered him, but he returned to the charge—

"Well, sir, perhaps there may be some mistake, but the likeness is very remarkable. Would you mind telling me who you are?"

"I don't think," said I, "that you have any right to ask that question. May I ask you, in return, who you take me to be?"

"Oh, yes," was the prompt reply, "Judge Wilson, of Long Island."

I winked solemnly, and saying, "No, my friend, you are wrong; but this is all a little too 'thin' for me," wished my chap-fallen interviewer good morning.

These attempts to impose upon me partly amused and partly annoyed me. The annoyance chiefly arose from a suspicion that I must look like a fool—a very painful suspicion it is needless to say.

One day a man accosted me near the

Brunswick Hotel, whither I was going to see a friend, and so took me off my guard that I told him the name of the ship in which I had crossed, and also the name of the captain. He begged my pardon and we parted. I thought this man really was mistaken. I went on to the Brunswick, and, my friend being absent, returned almost immediately. Almost on the spot where I had just been stopped I was accosted by a tall thin-faced man, with a fair moustache, faultless as to dress, and most voluble as to speech.

"How do you do?"

I stared blankly.

"Ah, I see you don't remember me. My name is Harry Jennings, and I am the nephew of Captain Jennings, with whom you came over in the *Adriatic*."

The names of "Jennings" and *Adriatic* had only passed my lips a few minutes before, a few yards from where I was now standing, and now they were uttered by another perfect stranger, who claimed my acquaintance as an old friend.

I saw through the scheme of the two confederates, and thought I would keep up the deception; at any rate, so long as it suited me to do so. My voluble companion talked incessantly, a nod or monosyllable of acquiescence being almost all that was expected of me.

It was a fine summer's afternoon, about half-past three. I had nothing better to do, and I had no little curiosity to see what the voluble one's "little game" was. He took my arm, and we walked across Madison Square.

"You will be glad to hear that since I saw you on the *Adriatic* I have been to Boston and won a prize in the lottery for the distribution of Longfellow's library, and I am now going to see if the books have arrived. The books, unfortunately, are both alike, but each has the poet's autograph. I shall only require one, you can have the other if you like."

I thought to myself this man must take me for a fool, and I felt half inclined to tell him so and leave him. However, I went on.

We entered a horse-car in Third Avenue, he kindly paying my fare. We got out at Fourteenth Street, a locality with which I was perfectly familiar, and went to a house about two blocks distant. A woman of the housekeeper class admitted us, and we turned into a room on the right hand with windows open overlooking the street. Behind a table sat a very thin, pale, well-dressed man. He gravely informed Mr. Jennings, with many expressions of regret, that the books had not arrived, but would be at his office next day. It seemed there were also some money prizes attached in some cases to the books, and Mr. Jennings inquired if he had been lucky enough to win one. The thin man, after referring to a large book, and to several smaller ones, replied that he had won 500 dollars, which he handed over to him. I was asked if I should not like to see how this lottery business was managed. I said, "Nothing would give me greater pleasure."

Unrolling a piece of oilcloth divided like a chess-board into squares, in which were numbers and gold stars, and producing a pack of cards, each with a different number (from one to thirty, I should think), I was asked to draw, on behalf of Mr. Harry Jennings, six cards. I complied, the numbers on the cards were added up, and resulted in a number

corresponding with one on one of the squares.
Jennings wildly congratulated me, and said
that I had won 2,500 dollars for him, which
he would share with me. I was asked to
draw again, and after one or two failures, the
causes of which were rapidly explained to me
with more than Mr. Jennings's usual volubility,
I again won for him 2,500 dollars. In both
instances a bundle of "greenbacks," fictitious,
of course, was handed across the table. Up
to this time I had not staked anything, and,
of course, did not mean to.

Mr. Jennings now tried to persuade me to
try my luck to the extent of the small sum of
11 dollars. If I lost, he would hold me
harmless, but he could not go on winning
unless I staked. He whispered confidential
remonstrances behind his hand, so that the
other worthy might not hear, and grew almost
angry at my obduracy.

At last I thought it time for me to ring
down the curtain, so I rose and said, "I am
much obliged to you. As a stranger I like
to see all I can. The ways of criminals have
a peculiar interest for me, for in my own
country I am accustomed to punish them.

You have lost some valuable time and 5 cents car fare; good day."

The two men stared at me open-mouthed. Neither uttered a word or attempted to interfere with my departure. The voluble man, whom I afterwards found was "Hungry Joe," one of the cleverest of the "Bunco" men in New York, was pale and speechless.

I was half inclined, at one time during the interview, to bring these two worthies into the clutches of the law, but discretion intervened, for although I knew very little of American police, I recollected that there was a prison specially reserved for witnesses whose presence at a trial was doubtful, and I feared lest I might involve myself in engagements which would interfere with my journey to the Yellowstone.

Returning to my hotel, I found a gentleman on the staff of the *New York Tribune* waiting to see me. To him I told my story, and he, from my description, at once recognised "Hungry Joe," as the voluble conductor of the enterprise, which, in my case, had failed so signally.

The next morning I awoke to find myself

famous! The *Tribune* published a very faithful and spirited account of my adventure, under the heading of, "A Bunco-steerer's wasted labour." My personal appearance, my peculiarities, my "aggressively British outward man," my "portly form," my previous history, were all described in a manner essentially American, and made me roar with laughter. I was the talk of New York. Nay, more,— afterwards as I journeyed to the Great North West, my approach was heralded by several of the local newspapers as the victorious hero of the great Confidence Trick: the article in the *Tribune* being reprinted either partly or *in extenso*.

The eccentricities of American newspapers might well form the subject of a separate chapter. American ingenuity is apparently inexhaustible in its power of inventing novel and sensational headings. I was told that on more than one journal, a member of the staff specially skilled in this art, is employed at a handsome salary to do nothing else. I will only mention two examples which occur to me. The body of an unfortunate suicide is discovered floating on the surface of the lake in which he has been drowned. One would have thought that the account of the Coroner's inquest would have been headed, "Suicide," or "Inquest," or "Found Drowned," or something similiar. No. The sensational writer preferred "The Floater," which, however correct in one particular, conveyed but an imperfect notion of what had happened.

Another heading struck me as peculiarly appropriate, and not altogether unworthy of adoption on this side of the Atlantic. A long list of cases and punishments in the Police Courts was entitled, "The way of the Transgressor!"

CHAPTER IV.

New York and its Food.

I shall never forget my feelings when a waiter bluntly placed before me for the first time a list of the food provided for breakfast—I cannot call it a *menu*—at the Fifth Avenue Hotel, and asked what I would take. The Fifth Avenue Hotel is a magnificent commanding structure of white marble, and is capable of accommodating a thousand guests. In every respect it is a first class house. Its decorations and appointments are most sumptuous, and the service and cooking excellent. It is admirably situated, overlooking Madison Square, in a conveniently central position, and is conducted on the American plan, as they call it, which really is very similar to the *pension* systems of the Swiss Hotels, though on a more expensive and luxuriant scale. The guests may partake of as many meals as they choose between 7 a.m. and midnight. Breakfast, dinner, luncheon, tea, and supper follow and overlap each other in rapid succession; so that whenever hunger seizes you,—if such an intruder as hunger is ever to be found in the Fifth Avenue Hotel,—you may instantly sit down to a "square meal" and extinguish him.

Perhaps it will be more convenient to let the catalogue of breakfast speak for itself, so here it is, premising that, as a matter of course, a large slice of water-melon, a bunch of Concord grapes, some bananas, or half-a-dozen peaches, are disposed of by most Americans to pass the time until the more solid viands arrive. These fruits are not included in the catalogue:—

FIFTH AVENUE HOTEL.

BREAKFAST.

BROILED.

Beefsteak. Tripe, plain. Pickled Tripe.
Veal Cutlets.
Calf's Liver. Smoked Bacon. Mutton Chops. Ham.
Mutton Kidneys. Pigs's Feet, breaded.
Spring Chicken.

FRIED.

Pig's Feet, breaded. Oysters, with crumbs.
Pickled Tripe. Calf's Liver. Tripe, plain. Clams.

STEWED.

Clams.   Veal and Mutton Kidneys.   Oysters.
Hashed Meat.

FISH.

Fried Codfish, with Pork.   Salt Codfish, with cream.
Hashed fish.   Boiled Salt Mackerel.   Smoked Salmon.
Digby Herrings.   Broiled Salmon.
Broiled Spanish Mackerel.   Fish Balls.

EGGS.

Omelets, plain or with Parsley, Onions, Ham, Kidneys, or Cheese, boiled, fried, scrambled, or dropped.

COLD MEATS.

Roast Beef.   Corned Beef.   Tongue.   Ham.

POTATOES.

Stewed.   Lyonnaise.   Fried.   Baked.
Fried Indian Pudding.   Oatmeal Mush.
Dry and dipped Toast.
Boston Brown Bread.   Muffins.   Rice Cakes.
Graham Bread.   Graham Rolls.   Cracked Wheat.
Corn Bread.   French Rolls.   Hominy.
Fried Hominy.   English Muffins.
Coffee, Chocolate, Oolong, Green and English Breakfast Tea.

Being of an experimental turn of mind, and doubting, moreover, whether all these various dishes could exist anywhere but in the "catalogue," I used to amuse myself by testing the capabilities of the kitchen. But it never failed, although I often did, to eat what I had ordered. One morning, while I was wondering what I should select, a very charming American lady of our party sat down to the table, and, scarcely glancing at the "catalogue," knowing, in fact, by experience what there would be in it, she said to the "boy,"

"I don't feel as if I could eat much this morning, but you may bring me some oatmeal mush, some tender loin steak and fried potatoes, some fish balls, some chicken hash, some corn bread, some griddle cakes and maple molasses, and some dry toast."

If she had taken the trouble to read the *menu* she would have seen that she had not quoted accurately, but the "boy" understood her, and soon returned with a multitude of small, oval, shallow, open pie dishes, in which reposed the several viands or the equivalents. But you must not suppose that she ate all these things. She ate of them. She sat with a square yard of table cloth covered with these various dishes before her, and, like a well known lady of fiction, she "dodged about among the tender pieces with a fork." She left more than half of what she had ordered, following therein the usual American fashion. The waste food of a large New York Hotel, conducted on the American plan must be enormous, and it is to be hoped that it is not entirely sacrificed, but is turned to some use.

Delmonico's disappointed me. Perhaps its reputation is so great that it has become careless. Or perhaps the proprietor, having amassed a large fortune, has ceased to keep that strict personal supervision which is so necessary in establishments of that sort.* One peculiarity, however, could not fail to be remarked, and that was the manner of the waiters, most of whom appeared to be French or Italian. In place of that abruptness which characterises the same class in America, these waiters at Delmonico's had a faint glimmering of the dignity of their profession, and took an intelligent and kindly interest in their customers' dinners, thus recalling, though remotely, the solemn *garçons* of the old " Trois Frères Provençaux " of long ago.

But if Delmonico's should be disappointing, the Hoffman House Café, the most splendid drinking saloon in the world, cannot fail to arouse feelings of astonishment and admira-

---

* Poor Mr. Delmonico! He was found a few months later frozen to death in the mountains near New York, whither he had wandered in a state of temporary insanity.

tion at the taste displayed in its arrangement, and at the almost priceless character of some of its works of art.

Foremost amongst these is a genuine Correggio of great value. Correggio, as is well known, usually painted sacred subjects, and only in seven instances did he select a mythological incident for his canvas. The Correggio at the Hoffman House Café is one of these, and is an undoubted original. The subject is Narcissus. There is also, among other pictures, a grand painting of " Nymphs and Satyr" of the French school, by Bougerreau; lovely statuary in marble and bronze, a large and unique piece of Gobelin tapestry made for Napoleon III., and a very choice selection of articles of vertu and rare plants. The chief pictures are handsomely mounted on crimson velvet, each with its special well-shaded electric light to show off its beauties to the best advantage. Having ladies in our party we hesitated to go in, and tried to obtain a view of the brilliantly lighted interior through the large uncurtained windows, but the manager seeing us, and that we were a party of foreigners, came out, and begged us all to come in, assuring us, as was quite true, that although the saloon was for men alone, still there was nothing to cause the least offence to ladies. If we had not accepted his invitation we should have missed a very great treat.

The traveller will rejoice, especially in August, over the abundance of ice which is to be met with everywhere in America. The severe and unvarying winters provide an unlimited supply, and arrangements for its storage are made on a gigantic scale. In public institutions, merchants' offices, clubs, hotels, steamers, railway cars, and private houses, there is always the capacious receptacle for iced water with its glass and drainer, which is free to everybody. The water of New York, supplied from the Croton river, is deliciously pure and soft, and although the New Yorker may possibly drink more of it when icy cold than is good for him, there is not nearly that consumption of stronger drinks with which the Americans are usually credited. Goblets of iced water are supplied *ad libitum* at every meal, and are amongst the most conspicuous objects on the table.

Before visiting America everyone will have

heard of clams, soft shell crabs, and terrapins. The terrapin properly cooked is a toothsome dish, but the clam is detestable; in fact I was told that the taste for clams was an acquired one. I could imagine a castaway on a desert island coming to love them so much as to enjoy them even without the usual squeeze of lemon juice; but in a country where food, and especially the oyster, is abundant, I cannot understand how clams ever obtained favourable notice. Perhaps they are better when cooked and eaten *al fresco* at a "clambake." The true clambake is only to be met with on the New England coast, where the clams are cooked in seaweed in a stone oven. But the raw uncooked clam is an unworthy dish wherewith to neutralise an appetite; and the soft shell crab is equally unworthy, more especially because it is uninteresting.

CHAPTER V.

SOME PECULIARITIES OF NEW YORK.

AMONG things conspicuous by their absence in the streets of New York are dogs. The visitor to that city will, after a day or two, begin to wonder, and to ask the question, "Where are the dogs?" And the reply he will get will surely satisfy him that I was right when I asserted in a former chapter that when the American authorities order any particular act to be done, you may rely upon their orders being carried out. There is something in this thoroughness and determination to "stand no nonsense" which is particularly charming to the Englishman, wearied by the hubbub and opposition raised on all sides in his own country whenever any decisive step, no matter how useful, is taken which necessarily involves the treading on somebody's corns. Beyond a few very small pet dogs carried by ladies there are practically no dogs to be seen in New York after the 1st of June until the summer is past.

Every year at this season the mayor appoints the official dog-catchers, pound master, and other necessary persons to carry out the city regulations. Every dog not properly muzzled and led by a string is captured and taken to the pound, a temporary structure erected annually on the most convenient available site on the bank of the East river. Once there, if not redeemed, by payment of twice the amount the city pays the dog-catcher, within twenty-four hours, the dog's fate is sealed. He is put, with other companions in a similar predicament, into an iron cage, which is swung out over the water and then lowered into it until all its occupants are dead. Whether canine rabies is more common in summer than winter is a questien open to doubt. But the City of New York has made up its mind on the subject, and the streets afford an example that London might follow with advantage.

One of the wonders of New York is the East River Bridge. We in England know it better as the Brooklyn Bridge, a name which is never applied to it in New York. Brooklyn

and New York are two separate cities, divided
by a ship channel (for it is not really a river)
of great width. Brooklyn, "the overgrown
village," as it has been styled, is the third city
in point of population in the United States.
It is situated on Long Island, and is the capital
of King's County. Since New York absorbs
almost all the business, Brooklyn is left in
peace and quiet. To it thousands of busy
New Yorkers retire to sleep off the cares and
anxieties of Wall Street and Broadway. It
acts in fact as a sort of great dormitory for its
more active neighbour.

To avoid the inevitable rivalry between the
two cities as to which should give its name to
the magnificent Suspension Bridge which connects them, it was better to let the nomencla-
ture come from the channel common to both
which separates them, and therefore the
gigantic structure is known as the East River
Bridge. It is nearly 6,000 feet in length.
The central span is 1,595 feet from tower to
tower. The distance from each tower to the
anchorage of the cables on each side is 930 feet,
and the approaches together amount to 2,534
feet. The total length of the bridge is, there-

fore, 5,989 feet. It is 85 feet wide, and includes a promenade in the centre of 13 feet, two railroad tracks, and four waggon or horse-car tracks. From high-water mark to the floor of the bridge in the centre is a distance of 135 feet. It had only been formally opened for traffic on the 24th of May, 1883, a few weeks before my visit, and was consequently still an object of curiosity and interest to the inhabitants as well as to strangers.

By the way, the day selected for the opening ceremony, being the birthday of Queen Victoria, roused feelings of bitterness and jealousy among the more prejudiced Americans, of whom, it must be confessed, there are a few, although our beloved Sovereign is, with these insignificant exceptions, held in the highest esteem throughout the States.

It was a lovely Sunday afternoon when I went to see the East River Bridge, and the fine weather, combined with the holiday, caused a remarkable number of people to be bent on the same errand as myself. Along the footway in the centre an almost continuous stream of people poured each way without intermission. Everybody was in holiday attire. Many nationalities were represented, and were dressed (the women especially) in the distinctive costumes of their countries. Here were to be seen Swedes and Norwegians, Dutch, German, and Italian peasants, Armenians, Chinese, and, of course, Negroes. But, amid all this mixture of tongues, the one alone audible above the rest was the Irish brogue.

A few policemen scattered at long intervals sufficed to direct the two streams of traffic, and prevent them from interfering with each other. They did not waste words, and possibly did not mean any incivility, but if any one encroached beyond the imaginary boundary of the space allotted to his stream, the policeman would point with his truncheon (always, it may be remarked, suspended from his wrist), and in a gruff, commanding tone, would say, " Here " or " There."

I endeavoured to make an approximate calculation of the number of individuals on the bridge that Sunday afternoon, and I concluded that, at a moderate estimate, there could not have been less than 15,000, and there were certainly not twelve policemen to preserve order. Yet, these preservers of order were unnecessary, and only issued their monosyllabic commands for the sake of doing something to earn their pay. Every one of these 15,000 persons was as anxious to preserve order as the constables.

There was none of that "rough" element which is the pest of all public and popular sights in London. Very likely watches and purses were no more safe there than with us under similar circumstances; but the respectable, well-to-do, happy appearance of the crowd, and its quiet and orderly behaviour could not fail to attract the notice of a stranger from London.

The policemen deserve a word of notice in passing. They lack entirely that compact, semi-military, business-like character, which more or less distinguishes the whole of our metropolitan force, from the A Division downwards. As a rule, the New York policeman seems to have been selected because he is tall, badly-proportioned, and not well set-up. Judging from his sleek shaven face, I should say that he got his share of the good things of this life. I was informed that each ordinary constable, or "patrolman" as he is called, receives from 800 dollars to 1,000 dollars per annum—*i.e.*, from £160 to £200, and that the entire force numbers about 3,000 men   The absence of smartness in the New York policeman is aggravated by his dress. He wears a badly-fitting, greyish-blue uniform, with a coat much too long in the skirt. He has turndown collars, and necktie of such pattern as pleases himself, and his head is covered by a grey felt helmet, round which is fastened a twisted silk cord tied in a knot, with tassels at the end. It is possible that he may be a very terrible person in the eyes of the *gamins* of New York, but to me he was rather a joke than otherwise.

I had not been in the city many hours before I received cards informing me that the courtesies of the two great opposing political clubs—the Union League and the Manhattan—had been extended to me, and I was welcome to use them during my stay.

My first visit was to the Union League Club, which is situated in Fifth Avenue, at the corner of Thirty-Ninth Street, and to which I had been introduced by Mr. Quintard, the President of the Club, I was duly shown over the building, and was much impressed by its size and the comfort of its arrangements. It is very magnificent, but decidedly dark, which darkness is much increased by the heaviness of its decorations, and by the handsome coloured glass which seemed to be always obscuring the light exactly where it was wanted. The offices are all at the top of the building, but a couple of "lifts," or "elevators" as they prefer to call them, in constant work, make access to these offices very easy. The spacious kitchen, laundry, butler's pantry, with glass, china, and plate cupboards, all most carefully and systematically arranged, well repay a visit. The large number of bedrooms for the use of members surprised me. There are no less than thirty-three, eleven on each floor below the offices. There are also many private dining-rooms, drawing-rooms, writing-rooms, cosy smoking-rooms, a spacious library, and in the basement a billiard-room with eight tables, a café, and a large bowling-alley, which when in full play must resound all through the building.

The Manhattan Club is also in Fifth Avenue, at the corner of Fifteenth Street. This is the

Democratic Club, and although not to be compared with the more magnificent Republican establishment, is more quiet and home-like.

The Union League Club must not be confounded with the Union Club, which, besides being non-political, is the most exclusive of the New York clubs.

The love of decency and order, to which I have alluded, is shown in many ways, but in none more than in the fact that the great open squares of New York, such as Madison Square and Union Square, are available at all hours of the day and night without offence to any one.

Madison Square, bounded on one side by Broadway, consists of about six acres, and is completely open, without any railing, to the public. Broad asphalte pavements run in every direction among the grass and flowers, and there is a fountain and fine shady trees, among which are dispersed innumerable comfortable benches divided by low arms into separate seats, for in this country of equality everybody is entitled to his share and no more. High in the centre is a lofty pole, at the summit of which is a group of electric lights, which cast a lovely light, brighter than moonlight, over the scene and make of it a veritable fairyland. In London such a place after dark would be a perfect den of abominations. In New York it is a charming public garden, where any one may sit or walk and enjoy the cool of the evening without the smallest annoyance.

Union Square is the same, only it is half the size.

It must be remembered, however, that these squares do not immediately adjoin the districts inhabited by the evil-disposed classes.

CHAPTER VI.

NEW YORK THEATRES AND PRISONS.

A VISIT to the Madison Square Theatre is a treat that cannot fail to be appreciated by the London play-goer. This theatre stands alone in the world in one respect—it has a double stage. There are two stages, one over the other, which are elevated or lowered as occasion requires. While the action of the play is proceeding on one stage, the scenery for the next act is being carefully set on the other stage. When the curtain drops, the stage, in a few seconds, is moved bodily up or down, and the next act is ready. Of course the plays have to be written for or adapted to the theatre, for there is naturally no provision for changing scenes during an act; and also a stage constructed on this plan must necessarily be limited in size. You could scarcely have it at Drury Lane, for example. This arrangement specially suits an American audience, for our cousins are not noted for patience, and do not like long "waits" between the acts.

When the orchestra begins to play, you wonder whence the noise comes. There is not a fiddle visible in the usual place. At last you discover that the musicians are placed in a beautifully artistic balcony in the arch over the intensely æsthetic curtain. I need not say that the effect is admirable.

There is another improvement which we in England might adopt with advantage. After the final fall of the embroidered curtain, instead of the lights being lowered, the brown holland being brought out in haste to cover the boxes and decorations, and the audience being hurried out helter skelter for fear of being locked up with the watchman and firemen, the band performs a piece of music duly set down in the programme, and gives the finishing touch to the performance by "playing the congregation out." I may add that this is the practice, so far as my experience goes, in all American theatres.

After the play Mr. Frohman, the manager,

took us over the theatre, and with great courtesy showed us the working of the machinery behind the curtain. We sat in the stalls while the stage was moved up and down, and all necessary connections of gas and water made. There was a considerable stream of running water in one "set," but it was managed without any appreciable delay. The ventilation was also elaborately perfect, and could be adapted for either hot or cold air. At the time of my visit cold air was largely in demand, so it was conducted over huge blocks of ice, and directed by means of multitudes of pipes underneath every seat in the auditorium, being thus distributed without creating any draught, while the foul air was drawn off from above. The result was that the theatre on that hot summer night, was really cooler and fresher than the outside air, although I entered it after the large audience had been seated some time.

The plays produced at the Madison Square theatre are commonly domestic dramas, which are selected with care to exclude everything in the least degree objectionable from a moral point of view. In fact, the proprietor has one chief object before him—namely, to elevate and improve the public taste.

The play-bill ought not to be overlooked, for it is a fine specimen of colour-printing, and worthy to be carried away as a pretty memento of a pleasant evening. It furnishes an example of the novel use of English words, or their substitution for others more familiar, in the following notice :—

"THE INTERMISSION BETWEEN EACH ACT
WILL BE FIVE MINUTES."

The law of the State of New York requires all managers or proprietors to print on their play-bills ground plans of each floor of their theatre, with the routes and points of exit distinctly marked. In the Madison Square theatre the safety of the audience receives additional assurance from the fireproof construction of the building, and the fact that the dressing-room and other work-rooms—all in their way models of comfort—are in a separate building, entirely shut out from the theatre, and that the vestibule is large enough to afford ample standing room on its fireproof floor for all who can be admitted to the two galleries.

The Casino, at the corner of Broadway and

Thirty-Ninth Street, is another theatre worthy of a visit, chiefly, it must be admitted, on account of the novelty and beauty of its construction. Both externally and internally it is built upon Moorish models, some of the courts of the Alhambra having been almost exactly copied in the decorations. The ventilation is complete.

At the end of the performance three-fourths of the audience ascended either by the long winding stair, or by the "elevator" to the roof, where a novel spectacle presented itself. The entire roof was turned into a summer garden, open to the heavens, and there, scattered about at little tables placed among the shrubs and flowers, and listening to the music of a large orchestra, the people sat and smoked, and took light refreshment.

The general equality of station and fortune among Americans produces its result in the theatres. Beyond a few proscenium boxes, which, however, are quite open to the public gaze, there is nothing to remind one of a London theatre. There are no stalls or pit. You enter in the centre at the back of what would be our dress circle, and from thence the floor slopes gradually down to the stage, and is covered with fixed chairs, at one uniform price of one dollar and a half if bought at the box office, but two dollars (or any sum according to the demand) elsewhere. The front rows of the balcony overhead fetch the same price. A wide passage runs down the centre, affording easy access to the chairs on either side and greatly facilitating exit in case of fire.

It is a sad breach of good manners in the United States to stand up, turn your back upon the stage between the acts, and survey the rest of the company through your opera-glass. A Viennese friend of mine did it at Chicago on one occasion, and was utterly at a loss to comprehend the cause of all the noise and ironical cheering which he heard on all sides. I and some friends witnessed the whole proceeding from a box and were convulsed with laughter. The more our friend gazed around through his opera-glass to discover if possible the cause of the disturbance, the more noisy the audience became, until at last, sublimely unconscious, he resumed his chair, and the hubbub ceased. But he never could be brought to believe that he had been the culprit.

Whether fashion varies in New York with the season, I cannot say, but my experience in August and September was that evening dress for either men or women at theatres was practically unknown. At the Star Theatre, where Mr. Irving afterwards appeared for the first time on an American stage, I found myself alone, among a crowded audience, in a dress coat and a white tie. The only persons to keep me in countenance were the checktakers of the theatre and the waiters at my hotel! After such an experience, I did not hesitate to fall in with the American custom, and do at New York as New York does. The American women are given to wearing large hats, with an abundance of ostrich feathers, and consequently they somewhat interfere at times with a good view of the stage.

While making these comments on New York it may not be without interest to let the other side have a word, and hear what the intelligent American thinks of some features of our dear old smoky London :—

"We took up our abode," said my friend—let us call her Mrs. Boston—" at one of your best private hotels, frequented by your best people. The street, which led out of Piccadilly, was narrow and gloomy, the weather was foggy and brown. The rooms were dull, the furniture heavy and dark, the carpets were shabby, and the wall-paper depressing. The lights—a pair of candles—only made darkness visible, and failed to illuminate the room. We had endless trouble on our way from the ocean steamer in looking carefully after our luggage ourselves, for you have none of our convenient system of checks. However, by dint of much fatigue of body and anxiety of mind, our bags and boxes safely reached our bed-chamber, an apartment still more gloomy than our depressing sitting-room. The carpet was worn and dull, but we were not permitted to use it, for oilcloth protected it in front of the toilet-table and washing-stand, and wherever a foot was likely to be placed. Oh, how fond you English are of oilcloth! Yet can anything be more forlorn? Our dinner was served in excellent style, I must own, by the most respectful of waiters, a man of noiseless movements and a trained demeanour. Certainly in the waiting you beat us. The silver service was old and eminently respectable.

We felt almost a sense of awe at the large dish-covers, but when they were removed we found very little beneath. American appetites cannot feed on silver and china, however imposing in quality."

CHAPTER VII.

Hospitals and Asylums.

Having been furnished with a special permit from the Comissioners of Public Charities and Correction (a curious combination, you will say), I spent a most interesting day on the islands in the East River, but chiefly on the largest of them, Blackwell's Island, a long, narrow strip, extending from opposite East Forty-Eighth Street to Eighty-Third Street, with a channel on either side navigable by the largest vessels. On this island are the Charity Hospital, Smallpox Hospital, Penitentiary, Almshouse, Workhouse, Hospital for Incurables, Blind Asylum, and Lunatic Asylum for females. The island contains about 120 acres, and is chiefly of rock, from which the convicts have quarried the stone and built the several institutions above named.

A steamboat belonging to the Commissioners left the pier at the end of Twenty-Sixth Street at 10.30, and in little more than ten minutes we were at the first landing stage on Blackwell's Island. There were many people on board the boat, patients going to the hospitals, and friends going to visit, besides a large number of ordinary visitors from curiosity.

On landing I went direct to the Penitentiary, leaving the hospital for another occasion. I found that there were between 700 and 800 prisoners confined, whose sentences varied from one month to five years. The buildings are old and inconvenient, but the prisoners have in other respects not much to complain of. They are so well treated that they come back again and again, and generally arrange, if possible, to spend the winter there. Most of the cells are very small—8-ft. long by 7-ft. high and 4-ft. wide. In many of these cells two prisoners sleep, the beds being arranged like berths in a sleeping-car, one over the other. Instead of solid doors wide gratings are substituted, so as to insure ventilation. The convicts dine together, standing elbow to elbow at high tables.

I asked the warder who showed me the establishment if the prisoners had the same right as ours, of having their bread, &c., weighed to see if they have the correct number of ounces allowed by the prison scale of dietary.

"No," he replied, with a smile at the absurdities of English prison management. "If a man wants more bread he has only got to hold up his hand, and it is brought to him by a warder; but if he was fool enough to complain of his dinner he'd just be told to go right away, and he'd get no dinner at all that day."

I found nothing worthy of special mention in the course of my walk through the Almshouse, Incurable Hospital, and Blind Asylum, where there were only very few blind persons. The Workhouse, however, had some points of interest. And first let me explain that "Workhouse" in America means what its name implies, a place where people are made to work against their will. The helpless, aged poor, live in comfort at the Almshouse; but the Workhouse is a place of punishment for minor offences, drunk and disorderly persons, women who misbehave in the public streets, men who desert their wives and families, and other misdemeanants. It is, in fact, a branch of the Penitentiary, and the prisoners in the two establishments do all the work of the island. At the time of my visit there were 450 men and 650 women in the Workhouse, and in addition to these about 1,000 of both sexes who had been transferred to do other work of the department elsewhere.

I was shown over the building by an old man apparently about 70, but actually within a few weeks of 80 years of age. His manner was gentlemanlike and dignified, and he had evidently seen better days. I was led by these considerations to ask him how he came to be in such a place.

He told me he was a Southerner, who had been ruined and reduced to poverty by the War of Secession. "I was too proud to beg," he said, "I had nobody to help me, I was too old (60) to get employment, so I 'committed' myself here, and have been here ever since."

He has been kindly treated and allowed many privileges, among them being that of showing visitors over the establishment and taking charge of the lending library for the use of the inmates. In fact he himself was largely instrumental in getting up the library, and he has the whole of the books and registers in excellent order.

At the Lunatic Asylum, which is for female patients only, I was most kindly received by Dr. Franklin, the medical Superintendent, who gave me into the charge of Dr. Emmett C. Dent, the principal assistant physician, to show me everything about the place. The buildings, like the Penitentiary, are old and inconvenient, so that I was not able to learn much that was new or useful to me.

There were 1,457 patients in the asylum, and the average cost per head is 1s. a day. Economy has to be most carefully practised, for the money granted by the city is barely sufficient, and is doled out with a very sparing hand. But Dr. Franklin cheerfully encounters all his difficulties and vanquishes them.

A very large proportion of the patients are Irish, and, in fact, British subjects form nearly one half (48 per cent.) of the inmates. Very few patients are under restraint. To prove this, Dr. Franklin sent a messenger to each of the twenty-eight wards unexpectedly to ask at each door, "How many patients have you at this moment under restraint?" The answers were soon brought back duly signed by the attendant in charge. Out of 1,457 patients only five were under restraint.

Entertainments of various kinds, musical and dramatic, are furnished by the kindness of friends, and occasionally the patients are treated to an excursion on a steamboat belonging to the department.

The "Code of Rules and Regulations for the Government of those employed at the Asylum," prepared by Dr. Franklin himself, afforded me much amusement by the terse common sense which marks its composition, and the singular quaintness with which the worthy doctor enunciates his views.

"All duty among the insane," says Dr. Franklin, "is responsible and respectable, but arduous, confining and teasing. The self-indulgent should never undertake it. The mentally or physically unadapted should never be encouraged to continue. The unbendable, the querulous, and the shirkers should be cut off. *Then* all who stay may be trusted, encouraged, and advanced."

The Doctor is especially anxious that the delusions of patients should not be humoured or encouraged. They must, on no account, be addressed by the titles which their disordered fancies lead them to claim. On the contrary, they are to be dealt with truthfully and honestly, in order to win that confidence which " lies close to the root of discipline."

As examples of quaintness of expression, I may quote from the " Rules for Attendants."

Their dresses are to be neatly and plainly made, " without trail," and on no account are they to " use window-sills as clothes horses!"

CHAPTER VIII.

The Immigrants at Castle Garden.

Castle Garden, where the immigrants are received on landing, is well worth a visit. It supplies abundant evidence of the care which the authorities take of the thousands who come to seek a home in the New World. It is no exaggeration to say that the State is ready to stand *in loco parentis* to the immigrant. Nay, no parent could be so potent in protecting these poor people.

Castle Garden was originally a fort, afterwards converted into a summer resort, and among other things is celebrated as the place where Jenny Lind made her first appearance in America. It was first used as an immigrant depôt in 1855, since which time defects in the arrangements have been gradually corrected, and now it would be difficult to imagine anything better adapted for the purpose for which it is intended.

The cost of its maintenance is about 150,000 dollars a year, and it is managed by a commission of nine members, six being appointed by the Governor, the other three being *ex-officio* —the Mayor of New York, and the Presidents of the Irish Emigrant Society, and the German Society. A tax of half-a-dollar a head is levied on all immigrants, and is paid by the Steamship Companies. This tax used to be one-and a-half dollars per head, and was collected by the State of New York, but a recent decision of the Supreme Court determined the illegality of this tax as being " a regulation of commerce, and, as such, a usurpation of the powers of Congress." The tax is now collected by the Federal Government, and handed over to the State Government, which makes good any deficiency if the cost of maintenance exceeds the amount received. One result of this decision has been the commencement of actions by the Steamship Companies to recover the sums illegally paid by them during previous years. Although the Statute of Limitations will bar this demand to a considerable extent, the amount claimed is enormous.

When I visited Castle Garden the *Helvetia*

had just arrived, landing 279 immigrants. Among these were 12 Armenians from Turkey, who were the special objects of interest for the day, as there had been some difficulty in finding an interpreter for them. Any European language has its interpreters at the depôt, who are ready to speak to or write letters for the new arrivals; but these Armenians were the first of their kind who had come. However, the difficulty was soon got over.

I had the good fortune to be accompanied in my round of inspection by Mr. Forrest, one of the commissioners, and by Mr. Jackson, the secretary to the commission, both of whom were most anxious to supply me with all the particulars I required.

The circular red sandstone wall of the old fort still remains, forming a gigantic amphitheatre, covered with a light but substantial roof. Here, in various divisions, were the emigrants who had arrived that morning, chiefly Germans and Scandinavians, with some Irish. Their lighter baggage lay scattered about, yet all in order. The heavier packages of those who were going West, had been placed in an adjoining storehouse, duly checked and ticketed. Two of the Armenians lay on dirty striped Turkish rugs, spread over the baggage of the party. They were young men of 18 or 20, and their dark eyes seemed to look sadly at us as we passed.

In this amphitheatre the immigrant finds a broker who—being under conditions which make fraud impossible—will change his money for him at strict official rates ; a railway ticket office where he can buy tickets for any part of the States; a doctor, if he requires one; and a restaurant where he can obtain plain food at moderate prices, but no beverages stronger than lager beer.

As many as 8,000 immigrants have been received here in a single day, but frequently 5,000 have passed through the depôt in that time. Between 7,000,000 and 8,000,000 have landed here since the establishment of the commission.

On landing, the immigrant makes an affidavit as to the circumstances under which he has left Europe, his family, intentions, and the friends, if any, who are willing to receive him. These matters are carefully inquired into before he is allowed to pass. A widow woman with half-a-dozen children and no friends, who would inevitably become chargeable to the rates in a few days, would obviously be rejected. A pauper demoralised by workhouse experience, would stand a very bad chance. Upon my remarking that in England we had found out that the taint could never be eradicated from the child born and bred in a workhouse, and that we were doing our best to obviate this, Mr. Commissioner Forrest became quite excited for an American, and appealing to Mr. Secretary Jackson, exclaimed,

"There now, is not that just what I am always trying to impress upon them?"

However, although workhouse paupers are justly dreaded, the immigrant without a farthing in his pocket, will by no means be rejected. I saw many of these waiting in the Labour Bureau to be hired.

There is no doubt that the Irish cause a great deal of trouble; they frequently behave so unreasonably.

For example, a few days before my visit, a family of assisted emigrants, an Irishman with his wife and a couple of children, had arrived and stated that they had friends in

New York anxious to receive them. On enquiry this was found to be correct. The friends came, received them with open arms, and vowed to do all they could for them. The same evening other Irish friends came in to see the new arrivals. Whiskey was produced. One of the visitors contemptuously styled the new arrivals, " Government paupers." Retort followed, ending in a row, in which the friends who had promised so much in the morning took the most prominent part in belabouring the new comers, who were found battered and bleeding on the kerbstone by the police.

Especial care is taken of women and girls, and woe betide any man who has the temerity to misconduct himself with regard to them.

The boarding-houses to which the immigrant is recommended are kept under constant and rigid supervision by the commissioners. Those who wish to start at once for their destination are sent direct to the railway or steamboat, without any need to run the many risks of such a city as New York.

If a man is unlucky in his first effort to make a living, the commissioners will take him back and give him a fresh start ; and if he is ill or meets with an accident, he is received into the hospital on Ward's Island, where he is kept until cured, while if an operation is necessary, it is not performed except by, or in the presence of, one or more of the Board of Physicians and Surgeons, which consists of the first men in New York, who give their services gratuitously.

The Labour Bureau is a novel sight. In a large semicircular apartment, divided in half, I saw seated on each side about 200 men and women, in almost equal proportions, waiting to be hired. The women are in charge of a matron, and anyone hiring them must give a satisfactory account of himself, unless known personally to the office. While I was there a gentleman wishing to hire a domestic servant was sent back to produce evidence of his respectability. No charge is made to the hirer, and of course none is required of the immigrants, everything being done for them entirely free of cost.

I learned that 1,271 immigrants had been landed that day from seven steamships, and that not one of them had been rejected.

CHAPTER IX.

NEW YORK.—HELL GATE AND THE HUDSON.

"AND this is Hell Gate!" I exclaimed, with an enthusiasm which surprised an American friend on board the *Yosemite*, as that model steam yacht made her way through the disturbed water of the channel between Ward's Island and Long Island, and which is the connecting link between the East River and Long Island Sound. I had long wished to see this celebrated strait, which, like all places and persons connected with the War of Independence, had always interested me greatly.

The name of Hell Gate was not inappropriately bestowed on this dangerous rapid, formerly only navigable under very favourable circumstances by vessels of light draught. The harbour of New York can be entered through two channels, one by way of Sandy Hook and the other through Hell Gate.

Lord Howe settled an annuity of £50 a year on a negro pilot who brought the *Experiment*, a frigate of 50 guns, successfully through this passage when the Sandy Hook route was blocked, thereby reinforcing his little fleet most seasonably. It is recorded that when the *Experiment* was in the most critical part of the boiling channel, Sir James Wallace, the captain, gave some orders on the quarter-deck, which, in the negro pilot's opinion, interfered with the duties of his office.

He touched Sir James gently on the shoulder and said,—

"Massa, you no peak here."

Sir James felt the force of Sambo's remark, and interfered no more.

The passage of this 50-gun frigate through Hell Gate was a notable event at the time, but the memory of it has passed away. The United States Government, feeling no doubt that New York Harbour could be protected in this direction by other means than the sunken rocks which made Hell Gate dangerous, decided to free the channel from the obstruction. Engineers were employed from 1870 to 1876 in drilling the principal rocks and charging them with nitro-glycerine, and in the latter year the whole mass was exploded. The *débris* is at present in process of removal, and further excavations and explosions are intended, but the passage can now be safely navigated at all states of the tide.

Before starting on our journey of 3,000 miles into the Great North-West, our host, Mr. Rufus Hatch—kindest and most hospitable of men—gave us a sort of preliminary canter (if I may so call it) one day up the East River and Long Island Sound, and on the next day up the Hudson River to West Point and Newburg.

Mr. John Roach, the eminent shipbuilder of New York, not only placed at our disposal his beautiful steam yacht the *Yosemite*, but he and his son accompanied us. This was how I came to pass through Hell Gate.

The *Yosemite* is a very swift boat, and did her twenty to twenty-two miles an hour quite easily. The noisy fashion in which her captain greeted or hurled defiance at almost everything we met or passed was very amusing. He shrieked shrill whistles at one; he trumpeted deafening fog-horns at another; but when we passed Mr. Jay Gould's yacht the *Atalanta*, lying at anchor off Twenty-Third Street, he combined all the hideous noises in his power, and crowned them by the unexpected discharge of a brass cannon, the *Atalanta* returning the salute in due form, and with equal noise.

The Hudson River and its banks are classic ground to anyone interested in American history and literature. Here is Fort Washington, captured by the British in 1776, with all its garrison of 2,500 men. Here is Spuyten Duyvil Creek, where the sturdy old Dutch trumpeter was drowned in his attempt to swim the Harlem River, "in spite of the devil," (hence the name) as recorded by Washington Irving, and a little higher up the river is Sleepy Hollow, also immortalised by Irving in his "Rip Van Winkle." At Yonkers was fought a naval battle between British and Americans. Near here is the place where poor Major André was captured and executed as a British spy, and finally, amid lovely scenery, we arrive at West Point, famous in American History.

The cordial welcome accorded to us by Mr. Henry Cranston gave occasion for many goodnatured jokes, when our American friends were reminded that there was a time when any attempts on the part of " Britishers " to reach West Point, would have met with a most determined resistance.

When the *Yosemite* got back to New York, it was thought more convenient that we should be landed at the end of Twenty-Third Street, in which our hotel was situated. It was quite dark when the first boat was lowered from the davits, and the ladies were put into it. Presently, before it was filled, it was found to be filling in another fashion.

There were loud shouts of—

" You've left the plug out." " We are all wet," followed by a hurried disembarkation.

Even in such a well-regulated yacht as the *Yosemite* the usual mistake had occurred, and when the seldom-used boats came to be unexpectedly launched the plug of one of them was missing. It was well the mistake was discovered in time, for we were half-a-mile from the shore, and the strings of barges and the night-boats going to Albany, made the landing sufficiently dangerous without having the plug out of your boat!

The next morning at eight the various members of the "Rufus Hatch" party mustered at the Christopher Street Ferry, crossed to Hoboken, and left at 9.30 in a special train of Palace cars on the Delaware and Lackawanna Railroad for Buffalo, *en route* for the Yellowstone.

CHAPTER X.

A RAILWAY JOURNEY.—NIAGARA.

To call the structure on which we crossed from New York to Hoboken a ferry boat, does not convey at all an accurate idea of its nature and general appearance. It is more as if an enormous slice off the New York road, terminating in a covered shed with every comfort and protection from the weather, were transferred across the Hudson and joined on to the Hoboken road, close to the railway station, which was our destination.

New York being built upon an island, and a large portion of the population being non-resident, has necessitated the construction of ferries on a large scale, to convey daily backwards and forwards hundreds of carts and carriages and thousands of foot passengers. The North, or Hudson River, is a mile in width, and substantially built vessels are required to ensure safety to the passengers, especially when the winter months come and floating ice descends the river. On several occasions a ferry boat has been carried away, locked in the ice, half way down the bay before it could be extricated.

The railroad which was our route to Buffalo is known as the Delaware, Lackawanna, and Western Line, or more concisely as the Lackawanna Line, named after the pretty valley through which it passes. A railroad in America is not the thing apart which it is with us. It is not built high upon arches; it does not burrow underground. On the contrary, it forms part of the daily experience of ordinary life among those whose means do not enable them to live in more favoured localities.

America is essentially a country of level crossings. The ordinary high road runs alongside or crosses on the level, as occasion may require. The inhabitants sit at their front doors to see the arrival of the train. The children play in the gutters on either hand. There are accidents every now and then, no doubt, but in America you must look out for yourself. Occasionally a train smashes up a street car which gets in its way. But that is a detail. On the whole, the plan does not work badly.

On an American railway every engine is provided with a large, deep-toned bell, placed on the saddle of the boiler. To this bell is attached a cord, which connects it with the little glass and metal apartment in which the engineer and stoker are sheltered from the weather. Before an engine is set in motion a few strokes of the bell give warning of its intentions, and so long as the machine moves about within the limits of a station, or at a junction, or in fact where there is any possible risk to human beings, the solemn tolling of the bell is kept up. After this warning the engineer would not be held responsible if he ran over any heedless unfortunate.

The result of all this tolling of bells is that the traveller, on first arriving at a railway station, naturally thinks that some religious services are about to be carried on in numerous churches and chapels, in and about the depôt. But the most weird effect is produced, when, courting sleep in vain, in the small hours of the morning, you are travelling express speed and meet another train, whose engine-driver blows his whistle and rings his bell as he rushes past you in the darkness. The mixture of solemn toll with wild, discordant shriek, is the most unearthly combination of sounds that can well be heard at such a moment.

A special train of Pullman cars awaited us, and *punctually at 9.30 we started. The Lackawanna line passes through some lovely scenery, mounting the ridges of the Alleghanies, or "Kittatinny," as the Indians used to call the great ridge running north-east and south-west for hundreds of miles. Advantage has been taken of the Delaware Water gap, where that river cuts the chain and makes its way to Philadelphia, to carry the railroad through the chasm, whose sides tower up to a height of 1,500 or 1,600ft.

As the day wore on we mounted higher, until the magnificent expanse of the Genesee Valley opened before us. We gazed in admiration as the cars hurried along, until, after a lovely sunset, darkness suddenly settled down upon us.

We arrived at Buffalo at 9.30, having

occupied exactly twelve hours in our journey of 450 miles across the State of New York.

Early in the day we had stopped for a few minutes at Scranton, a town which has rapidly sprung into existence in consequence of the enormous output of anthracite coal which abounds in that locality. Here a sad accident happened to one of our party, but happily was not so serious as it might easily have been. The train having stopped long enough for a dozen of us to get down, suddenly moved on for a hundred yards or so. A gentleman from Boston, thinking he was going to be left behind, made a foolish attempt to get "on board," and, missing his step, was hurled violently against a truck, with the result that his head was cut open for six inches. Luckily it was only a scalp wound, but the sight of a fellow-passenger with blood streaming from his head, partly carried and partly led into a waiting-room, acted somewhat as a damper on our spirits at the commencement of our great journey. However, it was the only mischance which we encountered from beginning to end. The injured man of course had to be left behind, but he was well cared for, and was able to return home in a few days.

Buffalo, at the foot of Lake Erie, is a great centre of commerce, and has splendid docks, wharves, wide streets, handsome public buildings, and most luxurious hotels. At any rate, I can vouch for the Genesee Hotel as a model of luxury and comfort.

Only stopping for the night, we pushed on next morning to Niagara, about twenty miles away. Of course I thought that, like many other places about which one has heard such lavish praise, I should be grievously disappointed when I saw it. Not at all. I don't believe it possible for any description to exaggerate the glory and loveliness of Niagara. Nay more, the longer you look at it the greater must be your admiration.

Photographs of the Falls are simply gross libels. They naturally convey not the smallest notion of the dazzling white foam, the delicate tints of blue varying from pale cobalt to deep indigo, the vast cloud of spray now carried here, now there, as the wind takes it, nor any of the marvellous atmospheric effects which fascinate the beholder.

You can sit and watch Niagara for hours, as the wondrous rapids hurry on in haste to pour their waters over the ledge of the Horseshoe Fall, and then, as if satisfied with their work, or stunned by the descent, roll lazily away from the cataract, until compressed by the narrowing gorge, and quickened by a more sloping bed, they exert themselves again, and rush madly along past the spot where that poor infatuated fellow, Captain Webb, blinded by his vanity, madly courted certain death.

Any one, with a grain of common sense, must see at a glance that the bed of the river where Webb was last seen is covered underneath the boiling torrent with gigantic blocks of stone, which must inevitably slay anyone who failed to float on the surface like a cork. Besides, the force and violence of this awful Malström must entirely take it out of the power of the cleverest swimmer to regulate his movements. The guides point out the exact place where Webb threw up his arm and went down, either sucked under by the tossing breakers, or carrying out his mad scheme (as is supposed) of diving past the most difficult and dangerous portion of the passage. There could only be one result. His body with the life beaten out of it was found in the awful whirlpool below, where the dark green waters slowly collect their scattered senses before moving steadily along towards Lake Ontario.

It would be an old story to tell of the height, width, depth, speed, volume of water, and such like details of the Falls. Have not these matters been amply set forth over and over again?

Everybody has heard also that the American commercial spirit has shown itself so powerfully, that every part of the American shore from whence a view of the Falls can be obtained has been bought up and turned into an exhibition, with an exorbitant entrance fee. It is only on the Canadian side that a view of Niagara can be obtained free of cost. The same grasping spirit, however, is not entirely absent on our shore, many important points, such as the Rapids and the Whirlpool, having been seized upon by speculators.

The electric light is employed at night to illuminate the American Fall and Goat Island with moonlight and coloured effect. This, to my mind, was almost a desecration. Fortunately the great Horseshoe Fall was too far off to catch any rays of this unworthy Vauxhall illumination, and thundered grandly in the darkness.

The Clifton House Hotel on the Canadian shore is undoubtedly the best place to stay, commanding as it does an uninterrupted and perfect view of the Falls. It has the advantage also of being just far enough to escape the wetting of the spray, which is an important consideration.

CHAPTER XI.

Chicago.

The fascination of Niagara is enthralling; it is hard to tear yourself away from the fairy giant. Softer and deeper was the blue of the Horseshoe Fall, higher and higher rose the lovely veil of spray, until it floated away in misty rain a thousand feet in air, a brighter rainbow spanned the stream, when the morning came for us to leave.

Chicago was to be our next resting place, after a disturbed night spent in the cars.

Our route lay through the province of Ontario, along the Grand Trunk Railway of Canada. This portion of Western Canada is in the heart of the great lakes. It has Huron on the north, Ontario on the east, and Erie on the south, and it experiences all the chilling influences of these vast expanses of fresh water. Skirting the southern shore of Ontario as far as Hamilton, our train then turned due west by Dundas, Harrisburg, and Paris to Woodstock, where we crossed the Thames, and, following its right bank past Westminster and Dorchester, we arrived at London. Here we were moved to another train, and taken past Lambeth and Hyde Park Corner to the frontier at Point Edward. This strange confusion of familiar names of places caused us great amusement.

We had now completed a not very interesting journey of 230 miles through British territory, but our return to the United States was effected in a fashion which quite compensated us.

By the time we got to Point Edward it was dark, which increased the mystery. Our entire train was moved slowly on board a gigantic ferry-boat in order to be ferried across the St. Clair River to Port Huron. The darkness, the swift stream, the shipping, the shore lights, and the heavy grunts and puffs of the engines of the ferry-boat, which was moved apparently by paddles, combined with a strange helpless feeling, when we were finally cast loose from the shore, all added to the novelty of the situation, and gave us an experience which was new to most of us.

Lake Huron is 250 miles in length, and 100 miles in width, and the St. Clair River or Strait, which forms the only outlet of the lake, is about 1,000 feet wide, the stream running four miles an hour.

When morning broke we were hurrying along over the levellest country I ever saw. This part of Michigan and Illinois is as flat as the lakes which adjoin it, and is little raised above their level. The railroad must have been constructed at little cost, for it only needed to lay the sleepers on the surface, and turn up the sides for ballast.

There is a saying that "All railways go to Chicago." And there is much truth in it. Its position on the west shore of Lake Michigan makes it naturally the great receiver and forwarder of Western produce, whether brought by land or by water, to the East and Europe.

Originally a small Indian trading station; the first brick house was built in 1833. In

1837 the population numbered 4,170. After the lapse of half a century it is estimated that Chicago now contains at least 600,000 persons. During the past year more than 20,000,000 dollars (£4,000,000) have been expended in the creation of over 4,000 buildings, many of which are as fine as any in the world.

The energy and enterprise displayed at Chicago is without a parallel in history. Before the awful fire of October 8th, 1871, had completed its work of destruction, plans were being prepared for rebuilding the doomed city. The greatness of the blow may be measured to some extent by a comparison with the Great Fire of London, which extended over 430 acres, while that of Chicago covered three-and-a-half square miles, and did damage to the amount of £40,000,000. Charitable help poured in on all sides to lessen the misery of the burned-out inhabitants, and offers of loans to help the work of reconstruction were lavishly made.

Let me here record one out of many kindly deeds of my host, Mr. Rufus Hatch, whose early days had been spent in Chicago, and whose interest in the welfare of its inhabitants has never ceased.

Knowing that an old friend had lost his house and everything it contained, including a valuable scientific library, "Uncle Rufus" wrote from New York saying that he had, unknown to his friend, been carrying on a little speculation in shares on his behalf, charging him interest for the money, and that now he had closed the account, and had the pleasure to hand him so many thousand dollars as the result of the transactions. I could relate similar instances of his unostentatious kindness which came to my knowledge, but this shall suffice.

The roadways of New York are none of the best, but those of Chicago, at least in the more frequented parts of the city, are bad beyond description. It is a singular trait of American character that while erecting palatial warehouses or private residences, they are content to approach them by streets by comparison with which a drive over hedge and ditch across country would be almost smooth.

The Grand Pacific and the Palmer House are the chief hotels in Chicago, and are two of the largest and finest in America. We were accommodated in luxurious style at the Palmer House, an establishment which deserves more than a passing mention. It has no less than 85,000 square feet (or nearly two acres) of marble floor, which conveys some notion of its size. The entire ground floor is open to the public, who, with the guests of the hotel, circulate freely throughout it. There is scarcely any need to go outside the precincts of the building for anything you may require. Here you may buy your railway ticket, have your luggage checked, your hair cut, your boots blacked. Here is a post-office, a billiard-room, a ten-pin alley, a barber's shop, a news-vendor's stall, a stationer, a chemist, a hosier and shirt-maker, a hatter, a cigar and tobacco store, a telegraph office, a bar, a restaurant, a coffee-room, a broker's office, a special stock and grain exchange, and, finally, here you may order what the Americans call your "livery," that is to say, any carriages or horses you may wish to hire.

Comfortable armchairs and spittoons are placed all around in nooks and corners, and here from morning to night men sit, or stand,

and talk, nearly all consuming tobacco in one form or another. It is a strange sight to watch all this from a conveniently placed balcony of the *entresol* of the hotel above, for the guests of the Palmer House live over all this, but, whether they ascend to the first floor by elevator, or by marble staircase, they need only pass through one corner of the busy scene.

In 1877 a wonderful piece of engineering was successfully accomplished in the raising of the massive iron roof of the Palmer House. The sixth story had been originally constructed lower than the others, being intended for servants' quarters. More rooms being needed, Mr. Palmer determined to raise the roof four feet, carrying up the walls. The roof of this great fire-proof building is most substantially constructed, entirely of iron and cement, and its weight is necessarily enormous. Five hundred jack-screws were used, being turned in unison to the sound of the foreman's whistle. Meanwhile the work of the hotel was not interrupted, the 700 or 800 guests in the house at the time knowing nothing of what was going on.

There is no lack of objects of interest in Chicago. You may drive through Lincoln Park, along the shore of the great inland freshwater sea, whose waves roll in with wildly foaming breakers when driven by a northerly gale—for there is no land in that direction for 320 miles—making fierce inroads into the roads and pavements that skirt the shore, and driving heaps of sand inland.

I should doubt if any city is better provided with parks and boulevards than Chicago. The area of the parks amounts in the aggregate to about 1,500 acres, and the boulevards, many miles in length, vary from 200 to 400ft. in width, the Avenue de l'Imperatrice at Paris having been the model which has been followed. Of course everything is not yet so completely "fixed up" as in the Old World, but both parks and boulevards are fine examples of landscape gardening, and at the date of my visit, the miles of flower beds were absolutely dazzling with colour.

Then, again, there is the waterworks' system, which is unique in its way. Unfortunately there is not much to see here except the great engines which pump the thousands of millions of gallons required yearly for the needs of Chicago. To obtain this water a shaft was sunk on shore, and from it a tunnel was run out two miles in a straight line into Lake Michigan. Through this "big bore," as the Chicagoans call it, the cool, clear, healthy waters of the lake find their way into the great well under the waterworks building. From this well the water is pumped to the lofty stand pipe, and so distributed through 500 miles of mains into every part of the city. This water is most delicious to drink, and a bath at Chicago is the very luxury of softness.

In a city which has suffered so much from conflagrations, the arrangements for the prevention and extinction of fires are naturally brought to a very high pitch of perfection, and, in fact, are not unlike a well practised pantomime trick. The moment an alarm of fire is given, a single turn of a handle liberates the horses, an automatic whip touches their flanks —not that it is needed, for these animals know their duty—the harness suspended over them drops on their backs, they walk to their places on either side the pole, the collar closes on their necks with a spring, the driver, who may

be sleeping in the floor above, is turned out of
bed and comes through a trap door into his
seat, and the engine is on its way to the scene
of destruction in less time than it has taken
me to write this.

CHAPTER XII.

Chicago.—Stock Yards—Pullman—Churches.

I don't know whether I ought to class the Union stock yards and their adjuncts among the sights of Chicago. They more naturally belong to the smells. The guide-books to Chicago are in doubt as to the meaning of the name, which, of course, is of Indian origin. One thing, however, is clear, the name "Chicago" has to do with bad smells. It is derived either from the wild onion, which grew profusely on the banks of the creek, or from the skunk or polecat, an animal supposed to have abounded here. The name seems to me prophetic, and, setting aside the onions and the skunks, I pin my faith to the pig-killing establishments at the stock yards as being worthy to have their awful stenches represented in the name of the city.

The bullock slaughtering is offensive enough to the eye and nostril; the all-pervading odour of cooked meat in the "canning" rooms is not without its merits as a good nauseating smell. But for a thoroughly abominable, appalling, and asphyxiating stink, the pig-killing department surpasses anything in my experience. Nothing would induce me to visit it again, neither do I care to dwell any longer upon it now. I will only add that among our party were some strong-minded ladies, whose thirst for knowledge apparently overcame all other feelings, and who lingered so fondly among the horrors of the place that the weaker sex (in this case the men) were in despair. At last we breathed the fresh air outside, and were congratulating ourselves on our escape, when, on turning a corner, a stench of a different character utterly confounded us. It was a heap of thousands of bullocks' horns sweltering and decomposing in the hot sunshine.

Perhaps it would be only fair to state that, notwithstanding my remarks on the odour of the "canning" department, I do not wish it to be inferred that there is any want of cleanliness, or even a suspicion of unsoundness, in the meat which is being packed up. On the contrary, the most scrupulous cleanliness pervades the place, and my confidence in the honesty of purpose of the great "canning" firms of Chicago is unshaken.

The bullock and pig slaughtering departments are, after all, only adjuncts of the great stock yards, and a visit to the one does not necessarily imply a visit to the other. The company owns 360 acres of land and forty miles of railway track, laid with steel rails, in connection with all the railroads entering Chicago. Only 175 acres are "under plank," as they style it, meaning, of course, "enclosed." A hundred acres are devoted to cattle yards, and seventy-five to covered hog and sheep pens. There are 1,200 cattle pens, sufficient to accommodate 20,000 cattle; 1,300 hog pens, capable of holding 150,000 hogs; 300 sheep pens for 5,000 sheep, and stabling for 1,000 horses. Fifteen miles of macadamised streets run through the yards, and forty miles of water and drainage pipes underneath, while more than 500 men are constantly employed. Six large artesian wells, varying from 1,100 to 1,200ft. in depth, provide pure water in abundance for every animal in the place. In the course of twelve months nearly 2,000,000 cattle and calves, and about 6,000,000 hogs, besides 750,000 sheep are received in these yards. Let me try to convey some idea of these numbers in another shape. If, for ten hours of every working day in the year, a constant stream of cattle at the rate of ten per minute, of hogs at the rate of thirty per minute, with the small addition of four sheep every minute, passed through these yards, it would fall short of the actual numbers brought to this market for sale, slaughter, or distribution!

All animals which are destined for the slaughterhouse are killed with a minimum of suffering to themselves, while all the live stock, whether for sale or slaughter, are made exceptionally comfortable while in the yards.

Our visit to the Stock Yards, as usual, had been made early in the day, so that we were ready by noon to go to Pullman, a town belonging entirely to the Pullman Palace Car Company, and "located" (as they say) eleven miles south of Chicago. Here are the extensive workshops, which on an average, turn out one complete Pullman Car every day. The workmen to the number of 2,500, with their families, are accommodated in houses, adapted to their various grades, but all neat, pretty, and comfortable. The total population is about 8,000, and every provision is made for the well-being and amusement of the inhabitants, but especially for their sobriety, the rules as to the sale of intoxicating drinks being very strict.

The magnificent Corliss Engine, (which supplies the motive power to the establishment) the water tower, the shops, the arcade, the library, and theatre, were visited and admired in turn.

The theatre is one of the most perfect conceivable, being a model of elegance and convenience. A visit to it would make Londoners very dissatisfied with what is provided for them. We were fortunate in having in our party the Misses Sophie and Fanny Robertson, and they most kindly tested the acoustic properties of the theatre by singing on the stage, as a duet, " Ye banks and braes." An excellent dinner, which followed at the

Hotel Florence, was unfortunately not honoured by the presence of Mr. Pullman, but in his absence we did not fail to remember his effort to reconcile capital and labour, and make the lot of the working man happier and better.

Mr. Emery A. Storrs, one of those humorists who are found only in America, convulsed us all by his speech in returning thanks for the toast of " Chicago." I only remember his concluding words,—

" Chicago," he said, " may now claim to be a civilized city. It has the three essentials, though many of you Eastern people may not be aware of it. It has gospel privileges, it has the *Atlantic Monthly*, and—it eats with a fork."

No visitor ought to leave Chicago without seeing one of the large grain elevators in full operation. This is not easy unless you are lucky enough to time your visit to the exact moment when the operation of unloading cars takes place.

The work is very swiftly done. The elevator swallows the grain like a hungry dog devours a mouthful of meat, and is ready for more before any more is ready for him. The train of cars usually runs inside what may be called the ground floor of the elevator, and their contents are shovelled out by machinery into the cellars, from whence the grain is "elevated" many stories high to the very top of the building, by means of scoop-shaped buckets, attached at short intervals to an endless band, running over drums. Having been "elevated," it finds its way into one of the vast receptacles, where it is weighed, and awaits such further disposal as may be ordered.

It is obvious that, having been raised to this height, it is the simplest of operations to cause it to descend down any of the numerous wooden pipes in any direction that may be desired. All the arrangements are most systematic, and every kind and quality of grain is kept quite distinct—nay, it is almost impossible that there should be any admixture or confusion of the property of different consignors. There are sixteen of these elevators, with a combined capacity of 18,500,000 bushels. The total receipts of grain of all kinds last year, were about 165,000,000 bushels. The number of vessels clearing the port (on the lake, of course) was about 14,000, with a gross tonnage of 4,750,000.

I have not hitherto alluded to the Churches of Chicago. There are more than 300 places of worship of the various denominations, and I was told that all were well attended. Of the Episcopal Churches, the most noteworthy are the large and handsome Church of St. James, the richly-decorated edifice of Grace Church, and the Cathedral, with its elaborate services and fine music. There was, however, one little Church which interested me above all the others. I refer to the Church of the Ascension, at the corner of Elm and La Salle Streets, on the North Side. Here the Rev. Arthur Ritchie, who is the Rector, is sorely exercising the minds of the Low Church party, by what they regard as advanced Ritualistic practices. One great cause of disagreement is that at the High Celebration at eleven, he does not administer the Holy Sacrament, but encourages, what he styles in the service book which he distributes, a "Solemn Mass when there is no Communion of the people." I had some conversation with him, and he explained to me that he preferred his communicants to attend the early celebration at eight o'clock, but he was quite willing, on receiving notice before service, to administer the Sacrament to any member of his congregation at the midday celebration. Mr. Ritchie, for this and other similar reasons, is somewhat in difficulties with his bishop. He is a very earnest, pleasing man, and has the power of preaching with great effect, but with a strong American accent and style, which, by their strange quaintness, are liable to provoke a smile from the Britisher. It is singular that the accent almost entirely disappears in conversation, and only manifests itself when Mr. Ritchie begins to preach. The ceremonial at the Church of the Ascension did not strike me as being very excessive. It was much less elaborate than several churches I could name in London. But the general effect, with white marble altar, surpliced choir, vestments, and lovely music, was very beautiful. The congregation was not large, but thoroughly devotional.

CHAPTER XIII.

The Northern Pacific Railroad— St. Paul—Minneapolis.

Our departure from Chicago was the real commencement of our journey into the great North-West. It was then that we found ourselves for the first time in the railway train which was to be more or less our home for the next three weeks, barring the time spent in the Yellowstone district.

Immediately behind the engine was a capacious car for our luggage and for the stores, fruit, vegetables, cases of champagne, claret, apollinaris, and lager beer, and other things necessary for the luxurious existence which we enjoyed. Next came the dining-car, with kitchen, pantry, store-room, and ten tables, five on each side, to accommodate four persons each. After that followed four Pullman sleeping cars, which were turned into drawing-room cars by day, and were furnished with all toilet necessaries; and after them the private car of Mr. John C. Wyman, of Providence, Rhode Island, the orator of our party—a gentleman of remarkable eloquence and geniality, always amusing us with some fresh joke or story. Finally, at the tail of the train was what is called an "observation" car, with a platform at the end where such travellers as did not mind dust, might sit and enjoy the scenery as we passed along. From this platform to the engine there was a complete thoroughfare right through the middle of the carriages, the only troublesome part being the crossing from carriage to carriage.

Punctually at 7.30 a.m. the serving of breakfast began, at one o'clock we had luncheon, and the dinner hour was six. We were about seventy persons, so we had to take our meals in two divisions. The "bed boys," or coloured attendants, who acted as chambermaids, began to make up the beds soon after nine o'clock, and by eleven everybody was fast asleep. It was a very strange sight to watch these darkies at their bed-making.

Their rapidity and dexterity were marvellous. Their civility and attention too, were beyond all praise.

At half-past-nine in the morning we moved out of Chicago and crossed the State of Illinois, 181 miles, to Rock Island, where we obtained our first view of the Mississippi, as we crossed the mighty stream to Davenport. The impression conveyed by this portion of our route, of a previously inconceivable expanse of level country, was very strange. Illinois has been very appropriately called the " Prairie State," for fully one third of its 55,000 square miles is composed of high level grassy plains, at an average of about 500ft. above the sea level, while the remainder of the State is much of the same character. At Davenport we were in the State of Iowa, and our journey from this point became slightly more northerly until we arrived at Cedar Rapids (259 miles from Chicago) when our route turned almost due north across the State. Cedar Rapids is a busy thriving place on the Cedar River, a tributary of the Mississippi, and is a good example of the rapid growth of towns in America in favourable positions. Thirty years ago it consisted of three houses. Now it contains a population of 10,000 souls.

It was night when we crossed the northern boundary of Iowa and entered the state of Minnesota, and as morning broke we were running steadily along through that State of many waters, as its name implies, and arrived at the important city of St. Paul at eight o'clock, having completed the journey of 529 miles from Chicago in twenty-two-and-a-half hours, including stoppages at Davenport, Cedar Rapids, &c. Our average pace was under thirty miles an hour—certainly not an excessive rate of speed, but we were delayed by what is technically known as " a hot box."

Our cars had each a name, such as Fargo, Minneapolis, Wamduska, Pyramid Park, or Billings. I happened to inhabit a section in the coach known as " Billings," a new and very comfortable vehicle. But, as often happens with new cars, one of the wheels worked stiffly and with a large amount of friction on its axle. The natural result of this was the over heating of thebox, and several times during the night the train had to be stopped in order to extinguish the flames. This bad behaviour on the part of "Billings" rendered necessary his removal from the train at St. Paul, and I and my companions had to be transferred to " Minneapolis," a steady and well behaved car, which gave us no cause for any further anxiety.

Mr. P. H. Kelly, Mr. Finch, General Averill, Dr. Sweeney, and several other leading citizens of St. Paul gave us a hearty welcome on our arrival. We found fourteen open carriages which they had provided for us, and in which we made the tour of the city, having all its leading features shown to us. Our long procession wound its way through the hilly streets and out into the suburbs, where we were amazed at the picturesque and luxurious residences which met our view on every side. One of my companions, who had not altered the time of his watch since he left England, remarked that, although the city clock showed it to be 9.50 a.m. at St. Paul, it was 4 p.m. in London.

St. Paul apparently sprang into existence because here occurred the first obstruction to the free navigation of the Mississippi. From the mouth up to this point, a distance of 2,070 miles, there is nothing to impede the traffic along the river, except the sand and mud banks continually shifting as the great river is flushed by heavy rains or diminished by drought. But about nine miles above St. Paul are the Falls of St. Anthony, where the Mississippi, a quarter of a mile in width, descends seventy-four feet, eighteen of which are perpendicular.

In 1837 the Indians ceded to the United States a small tract of land here and a military and trading station was established. Lumbering, trapping, and hunting were the only industries, and the only white population up to 1849 was that scattered about the military and trading posts and the mission stations. This year we saw a flourishing city, a great commercial centre, with its hotels, State capitol, Opera-house, public squares, and a population of 100,000 persons.

The Falls of St. Anthony, having, by their obstruction, given birth to one large city, soon, by their usefulness, called into existence another city almost, if not quite, as large. So important a means of water power could not long remain idle. Timber had to be sawn, wheat had to be turned into flour. The flour mills of Minneapolis and the superiority of their products soon became known all over the world. In 1860 they produced 30,000 barrels, in 1881 3,142,974 barrels. The entire wholesale trade—including flour, grain, and lumber—will this year reach to close upon 100,000,000 dollars. All this prosperity has had its effect on the rapid expansion of Minneapolis, which now stands almost within sight of St. Paul, each of the twin cities annually stretching out its arms farther and farther, and the time must soon come when the hands will touch—but not clasp. Oh, no; the rival twins are too jealous of one another. It is said that whenever that time comes, each will build a wall to exclude the other.

The city of Minneapolis is remarkable for its fine churches, residences, and public buildings. The Court-house, the Academy of Music, the City-hall, the Opera-house, and the University of Minnesota, are buildings which would excite admiration anywhere, but to find them in this infant city of the West calls forth profound astonishment. We had been welcomed here as at St. Paul, and I had the good fortune to be accompanied in my inspection of the town by Mr. J. C. Whitney, one of the original founders of the place. In fact, he was able to point out to me the house which he built thirty years ago, the first house ever built in Minneapolis. And now there are 100,000 inhabitants. It was indeed strange to be reminded that within twenty years, this neighbourhood was the scene of one of the most awful massacres by Indians ever recorded.

The State of Minnesota is in the centre of the continent of North America, and its elevated plateau is the highest land between the Gulf of Mexico and Hudson's Bay, and forms the water-shed of the three great river systems of the country. The surface of the State is an undulating plain at an average elevation of 1,000ft., except where a group of low sand hills, known as the "Hauteurs des Terres," rise to a height of about 600ft. above their surroundings, and form the dividing line between the Mississippi and Lake Superior, and between the Mississippi and the Red River. Scattered over the surface of the State are more than 7,000 small lakes, varying from one to thirty miles in diameter, while several of them have an area of from 100 to 400 square miles. The Mississippi rises in one of these, Lake Itasca, and flows, winding about, for nearly 800 miles, through the State, receiving the Minnesota at Fort Snelling, between St. Paul and Minneapolis.

We did not visit both the twin cities on the same day. It would have been too much in such hot weather as we were enjoying. After seeing St. Paul we took train to Minnetonka Beach, about twenty-five miles to the northwest. It is the favourite summer resort of the inhabitants of the two cities, of which it may almost be regarded as a distant suburb. Minnetonka Lake is one of the 7,000 to which I have just alluded. It has an area of twenty-three square miles, but so many are the bays and indentations that the coast line is one-hundred miles in length. There are no frowning mountains such as surround the Swiss lakes, only gently undulating land, richly wooded, encloses this lovely sheet of water. Everything is peaceful and suggestive of happy rest.

Here not so many years ago was the home and favourite hunting-ground of the Sioux and

Chippewa Indians, and the middle of the lake was the boundary between the two nations. It was they who called it "Minnetonka," or the Big Water. Now large steamboats, the largest capable of holding 2,000 passengers, ply upon it, and hotels and private residences are springing into existence in every direction.

The Hotel Lafayette, which was our destination, is a good example of the great American watering-place hotel. It is built entirely of wood, and is architecturally of the Queen Anne style. It was, when first completed, 700ft. in length, but it has been increased by 400ft. during the past twelve months. The ground on which it stands is not very high, and yet it is the highest in the lake's circumference. Shady walks, pleasant drives, boating and bathing-houses, and a spacious wharf for the steamers are among the many advantages offered. Of course, the electric light is everywhere.

As an instance of the enormous increase in the value of the land here, I may mention one island on this lake, scarcely an acre in area, for which the present owner ten years ago paid the Government price of 4s. (1 dollar).

He has recently refused £2,000 (10,000 dollars) for it. Here is " unearned increment " sufficient to make Mr. Chamberlain's mouth water, but of this he may rest assured that if he were to promulgate any of his views in the United States casting any doubt on the owner's right to the full market price, he would soon be taught a very valuable lesson.

CHAPTER XIV.

Fargo.

While surveying the surrounding landscape from the level plateau which forms the roof of the Pillsbury Mill at Minneapolis, with the thermometer at 85 deg. in the shade, I was told that if the flour produced by the establishment underneath our feet in twelve months were packed in railway cars, it would extend seventy miles in one direction, while the wheat brought in to produce it would extend seventy miles in another! This is one of those striking calculations which some persons are so fond of making, and the accuracy of which it is difficult to test. But I have no doubt my informant was correct, for the producing power of the mill is no less than 5,000 barrels per day. It is a saying in Minneapolis that if a man wants credit from his banker he must go to him with his coat well floured. I can only say that if that condition were all that a Minneapolis banker required, I was in a position at that moment to have successfully negotiated a very considerable loan.

Returning to St. Paul I spent the afternoon in trying to keep myself cool in a sweltering heat of over 80 deg. Our special train had to wait until the evening so as not to interfere with the ordinary traffic. As I sat in the train, melting helplessly and trying to fan myself with a newspaper, a boy in a local train that was just starting had his sympathy excited, and calling out " Here, take this," threw something in at my window. It was his fan. I was very grateful to that Good Samaritan of a boy. He deprived himself of something that was almost indispensable to his comfort in order to benefit the less-acclimatised stranger.

It was 8.30 that night before we started from St. Paul. We were now for the first time on the Northern Pacific Railroad, along which we were to travel for the rest of our journey west. When I left Chicago I was told that I must be prepared to "rough it," but at St. Paul and Minneapolis, hundreds of miles away, comfort and luxury of every kind (excepting always

H

good roads) still surrounded me. Many miles had yet to be traversed before the "roughing it" was to commence. It was a lovely night, the moon was full, and the ride over the prairie was very delightful. The air was singularly light and invigorating, and its coolness went far to restore exhausted nature after the oppressive heat of the town.

We reached the boundary of the State of Minnesota at daybreak, and at six o'clock our train came to a standstill at Fargo, on the other side of the Red River, just within the territory of Dakota. A board on the station informed me that we were 274½ miles from St. Paul, and 1,641½ miles from Portland on the Pacific Coast. There is nothing like being exact to half a mile when dealing with such distances. It was Sunday morning, and in accordance with Mr. Rufus Hatch's inexorable rule we were never allowed to travel on Sunday. Our train was switched on to a siding, and we prepared to spend the day.

Fargo is as remarkable in its way as any of the other important places we had passed. Here we found a city of nearly 12,000 inhabitants, with twenty-eight hotels (such as they were), with three daily and five weekly newspapers, a post-office, where eight mails arrive and depart daily, banks, waterworks, opera house, theatre, two skating rinks, and, literally to crown all, the electric light in full operation. From the summit of an iron frame-work 200ft. high, when night came, a cluster of electric lights on the Brush system of 20,000-candle power, shed their radiance on this prosperous little city.

We were received with great cordiality by the leading citizens, who did everything in their power to make us welcome. The mayor, Mr. Yerxa, had requested all who could place their carriages at the disposal of Mr. Hatch's guests to be at the Head-quarters Hotel at 5 p.m. to take us for a drive round the city. The president of the First National Bank was good enough to act as my escort, driving my wife and myself in his light spring buggy in all directions through the beautifully-wooded park on the banks of the Red River and out over the prairie, pointing out everything of interest. It was a strange experience, because often there were no roads worth mentioning, and our ideas of driving were considerably enlarged.

You had only to hold on at critical moments and you could go anywhere.

By the way, I was rather taken aback by finding that the fame of my adventure with the "confidence men" in New York had preceded me. In fact the *Argus*, the chief paper of Fargo, had that day, in anticipation of my arrival, republished the whole story as it had appeared in the *New York Tribune* nearly a fortnight before!

Colonel Donan, the editor of the *Argus*, is undoubtedly "one of the most remarkable men in our country," as his fellow-citizens said. He is unsurpassed in that style of writing and public speaking that is known as "high falutin." His " Scream from the American Eagle" has passed through more than ten editions, and is a wonderful piece of composition. It is a "Fourth of July Oration," and was reprinted by the Passenger Department of the Chicago, Milwaukee, and St. Paul Railway "as a characteristic specimen of the fertility of the new North-West in eloquence," with a recommendation to the reader "when through" to "pass it along" to his neighbour.

Boasting, as is essential on the 4th of July,

of the greatness of the United States, Colonel Donan refers more especially to Dakota in the following terms.

"No bigger mosquitoes were ever broiled and served in fashionable restaurants down East, as snipes on toast, than those that industriously ply their profession along all our romantic streams and lake sides. No sharper, nobler, wide-awaker, straighter tobacco-spitting, more enterprising, whole-souled, generous, true-hearted, and public-spirited men than ours ever left their stoga boot-prints on the golden sands of time," with much more to the same purpose.

But amid all this amusing nonsense, Colonel Donan does not fail to give some sound practical advice, as the doctor administers a nauseous powder to a child in raspberry jam. He appeals to his fellow citizens to make Dakota "a land of God and morality, of law, order, and the broadest liberty. Let the taper spire of church and school house be ever, as now, the first landmarks in all your towns."

Let me retrace my steps a little, for I have omitted to mention a fresh surprise which was in store for me.

After breakfast I determined to see what sort of a place the Episcopal Church of "Gethsemane" would be, and after plodding along the wooden side walks, which are the rule in these out-of-the-way places, I came to a very unpretending structure, of course, built of wood. To my amazement, on entering, I found myself in a beautiful little church of the best Anglican type. All the fittings, except a handsome stone font, were of pine wood, substantial, and in admirable taste. The sittings were free. There was a rood screen, prettily-carved seats for the choir, a lectern, and a neat pulpit. The altar was decorated with flowers and prairie grasses surrounding a brass cross, and was vested with a beautifully embroidered altar-cloth of green satin.

After service I had the pleasure of being introduced to the rector, the Rev. B. F. Cooley, and I then found that the seasons of the Church were duly marked by equally handsome altar-cloths of appropriate colours, one of the cloths having been given by a gentleman of New York, the others having been embroidered by members of the congregation.

Presently the organist played an opening voluntary, and, singing a processional hymn, a choir, twenty-six in number, all in cassocks and surplices, headed by a cross-bearer, marched in and took their places. I could scarcely believe my eyes. Here, in this remote spot, in the very heart of the American Continent, was a church and a service that was an example to scores of churches at home. Everything was done with the greatest reverence and care, and following the best traditions of the Anglican Church.

Mr. Cooley preached us an excellent sermon on the Good Samaritan, and made an earnest appeal for funds for the further enlargement of the church, which has already been enlarged once during his incumbency of only twenty-six months. Yet even now it only holds 200 persons, and then is crowded.* Mr. Cooley told me he had 150 communicants, and that he had a choral celebration once a month ; the usual

---

* During the six months which have elapsed since my visit, " Gethsemane " has been greatly enlarged, and the total capacity of the Church, inclusive of the Galilee on the west side, is not far short of 500 sittings. Every one of these sittings was occupied when Bishop Walker, of

early celebration at eight being plain. Gethsemane Church was built in 1875, two years after the first lots in Fargo were sold by the Northern Pacific Railroad Company. In 1872 Fargo was inhabited only by the wild Indian.

It was a very great pleasure to find the spiritual wants of our Church people in the Far West so well cared for, concurrently with their material interests, nay, almost in advance of them. The ground has been acquired for a Cathedral, and Fargo will be an episcopate before many months are gone.

There are slight but curious differences between our Anglican services and those of the American Episcopalians. But substantially, so far as I could judge, there was no material discrepancy.

The Lessons are read from the version sanctioned by the American Bible Society. Various amusing concessions are made to Republican prejudices. For example, "King

---

North Dakota, in whose diocese Fargo is, paid his Episcopal visit in February last. It was a notable occasion for the Episcopalians of Fargo, and Mr. Cooley had good reason to feel proud of the success that had attended his unfailing exertions.

of kings and Lord of lords," is changed to
" Supreme Ruler of the Universe." For some
reason or other, too, the good old Saxon word
" wealth " has been replaced by " prosperity."

There are forty-nine places of worship of
all denominations in Fargo. The Roman
Catholics and Lutherans are largely in the
majority in point of population, the Lutheran
element being due to the numbers of Scandinavians who settle in this locality.

I had some interesting talk with Father
Stephan, the priest of the Roman Catholic
Church at Fargo, a most zealous missionary
among the Indian tribes, and a great friend of
" Sitting Bull," whom he is said to have converted to Catholicism. He had a much higher
opinion of the Indian Chief than I had ; but I
reserve my remarks on Indians until a more
suitable opportunity.

We were off the next morning at half-past
eight, and soon covered the twenty miles
between Fargo and the celebrated Dalrymple
Farm, or rather group of farms. These farms
are divided into forty blocks of a square mile
each, but all have not yet been brought into
cultivation. Our train drew up, and we were

presently scattered over the prairie, some on horseback, but the majority in waggons. We saw the whole process of reaping, binding, and threshing on a large scale. Not that there was much novelty in that. What struck me most was, not the present production of grain, but the future possibilities under a different system of farming.

The Red River Valley, probably, in remote times formed the bed of a great freshwater lake. The surface soil is a rich, dark, calcareous loam, of great fertility, extending more or less to a depth of from two to five feet. It is only necessary to "scratch" the surface, sow the seed, and in four months you have a yield of from twenty to thirty bushels of wheat to the acre. Oats yield fifty bushels, and barley and rye do equally well, while potatoes grow to an astonishing size. As far as the eye could see there was nothing but waving wheat in every direction. Here and there on the horizon was a manager's house and homestead. The farming operations are directed by means of the telephone. The stalk of the wheat was short and sturdy, capable of bending to the stormy blasts that sweep over the prairie and recovering itself.

I was told that the only drink supplied on the farm was water, in fact I saw the cart going its rounds with barrels of water to quench the thirst of the labourers. The foreman, who drove me in his waggon, assured me he had been a total abstainer all his life. He also, in answer to my inquiry, informed me that their steadiest and most valuable workers were young Irishmen, adding,—

"Not those fresh from Ireland, but the next generation who have been born in America away from the large Eastern cities, and who have forgotten, even if they ever knew, all the nonsense about their old country."

These men come to Dalrymple for the summer season, and return to various other trades in more populous localities during the winter months. Indeed, only the few who are absolutely necessary remain on the farms during the winter season, when the temperature, which may have reached 100deg. Fahrenheit in July and August, descends to 20deg. below zero in January.

CHAPTER XV.

Across the Prairie— The Gros Ventres.

After leaving the great Dalrymple Farm district, the traveller by the Northern Pacific Railroad begins to have real experience of the prairie. He has seen prairie before, away East, but only on a moderate scale compared to the landscape that now meets his eye on every side. There is often little variation for miles and miles. It was much as if the Atlantic Ocean had become solidified, and we were crossing it in a railway train instead of a White Star steamship. At long intervals we passed or stopped at some station, adjoining a street with wooden houses, a National Bank, and usually a daily newspaper.

Surmounting the slightly elevated land which divides the Red River Valley from the great basin of the Missouri, we came upon the James River, which flows eventually into the

Upper Missouri, and we stopped at Jamestown, a rising city, in a district rich in agricultural resources, about ninety-four miles from Fargo. I was told that nine years ago four small shanties at the crossing of the James River marked the site of the city, which now boasts of a mayor, a public park, four banks, and five hotels, good schools, three fine churches, and two daily newspapers. Three years ago there were less than 400 inhabitants. Now, there are more than 3,000!

Fifty-eight miles more of prairie, varied only by here and there a settler's wooden hut or canvas tent, and we arrived at Steele's Farm. We were just becoming accustomed to the dreary, treeless waste of land, when our train pulled up at a pretty and prosperous settlement, blessed with most of the comforts of civilisation, always excepting afternoon callers to break the monotony of their existence. This defect was so amply supplied by our arrival that we seemed literally to take the place by storm. But the hospitable Steele family were equal to the occasion, and nothing daunted, offered us a hearty welcome and the best their house afforded. In the garden a hammock was suspended under a large umbrella, which proved that some one there either had, or expected to have, some idle time. The house, which, of course, had been sent from St. Paul or Chicago ready made and only requiring to be put together, was a pretty villa residence. Among the furniture a really good piano had not been forgotten. A charming old lady, with white hair, and her daughters received us with every well-bred grace and courtesy. The farm buildings were extensive, especially the arrangements for poultry, which were very perfect and on a large scale, for milk and poultry command high prices in this out-of-the-way region.

Still on and on over this eternal prairie! until one wonders how a railway came to be built where there are such sparse customers; where, in fact, there are no persons to travel until the railway plants them there. One thing is clear, the railway does not require much constructing. Lay the sleepers on the prairie and turn up the sides for ballast, spike the rails on the top, and the thing is done. Still labour is expensive and so are materials, for everything must be brought from a great distance.

To tempt speculators to build the Northern Pacific Railroad, and so open up one of the most productive regions in the world, a rich bait was offered. The United States Government, in order to aid the construction of this line, has granted to the company lands extending from the Montreal River, on the eastern boundary of the State of Wisconsin, to Puget Sound, in Washington territory, a distance of about 2,000 miles, and embracing an area of about 42,000,000 acres, equal in extent to England and Wales combined. The Government grant confers upon the company the odd-numbered sections (each section being one square mile, and containing 640 acres) for a distance of forty miles on each side of the road in the Territories, and for twenty miles in the States.

Writing in 1876, Lord Dunraven, describing his visit to the great Wonderland of the Yellowstone, says:—"'When the railway is made,' is in Montana a sort of equivalent for our phrase, 'When my ship comes home.' The Northern Pacific Railway was surveyed through the best parts of the Territory, and under the benign influence of that great civiliser Montana would rapidly have developed into a prosperous State. But the Northern Pacific came to an untimely end. No one but Providence and financial agents can possibly say whether it is ever likely to be 'put through,' and in the meantime the Northern Territories are steadily 'advancing backwards.'"

A few years only have passed, and now the railway is "put through," the last spike has been driven, and the days of prosperity foretold by Lord Dunraven are close at hand.

It was dark when we arrived at Bismarck, forty-three miles from Steele Farm, an important busy city, of longer standing than most others we had passed, because of its position on the eastern bank of the Missouri, with 1,200 miles of navigable river above, and 2,500 miles below it. Our train remained more than an hour at Bismarck, and we were honoured by a visit from Mr. Ordway, the governor of Dakota Territory, a gentleman whose courteous manners and noble physique seemed to justify his selection for the important post which he filled. After he was gone our train was moved on five miles further, across the Missouri River, to Mandan, where we remained all night, sleeping, of course, in our travelling hotel, the train. We had got through 200 miles altogether that day, which, considering our many and lengthy stoppages, was not very bad travelling.

Mandan is only about two years old, but its population numbers 1,500. At breakfast we were asked by newsboys to buy the *Mandan Daily Pioneer*, a flourishing journal, whose chief business is to chant the praises of Mandan. Its editor ask the foreign visitor to "gaze with mingled feelings of pride and awe." He assures us that "no place seems more worthy of a setting in the crown which the intrepid financier (Mr. Villard) so richly deserves, as a tribute from a grateful people whose prosperity has followed the advent of the steam-engine across the country, than Mandan, which was known three or four years ago only from a few log-cabins, through whose port-holes anxious eyes kept daily watch for the dusky savage, and which stands to-day a prosperous city of 2,500 people."

I think, by the way, that the figure "2" must have slipped in in place of "1," or else the editor's enthusiasm has made him see double. However, Mandan, which is a busy shipping point for Missouri River Steam Boats is, no doubt, progressing rapidly, and has a great future before it. Amongst other features of the place the eye is attracted by excellent buildings of red brick, manufactured from clay found on the spot. Foremost among these is the Inter-Ocean Hotel, a most comfortable and admirably conducted establishment.

We left Mandan soon after breakfast, and our next resting place was Richardton (eighty-five miles), a small town of fifty inhabitants, with streets duly marked out, and, no doubt, looking very extensive and important "on paper." In twelve miles further Gladstone was reached; and here, I believe, it was that we came upon a very shabby-looking party of Indians standing perplexed on the platform, hoping for a lift on their road west. They were of the Gros Ventre tribe, and were on their way to hold a "Pow-wow" with their friends the Crows. They carried a document, without which no Indian is allowed to travel from his reservation, giving permission to " Rabbit's Head," " Porcupine Head," "Kidney," and three or four others, all named, to be absent for twenty-five days from the Agency to visit their friends at the Crow's Agency. Mr. Rufus Hatch, kind-hearted as usual, offered them seats on the observation platform of the last carriage of our train as far as Little Missouri, about fifty-three miles further on. We all crowded to look at them, and some ladies of our party bought bracelets, bags, and pincushions, while an energetic French schoolmaster bartered knives with them for a tomahawk-head and a red clay pipe decorated with feathers.

In my boyhood I had almost worshipped the "Last of the Mohicans." Was his name Chingachgook or Uncas? I know somebody's name was Chingachgook. I had longed to clasp these noble savages to my heart, to sit entranced while I was addressed in solemn and dignified tones as "Pale Face." The realities of life have extinguished nearly all the romance which I ever had. But I still clung to the noble savage of Fennimore Cooper's novels. Alas, now all is gone. Those hideous, dirty, sly-looking imbeciles, the "Gros Ventres" have to answer for this.

All on board the train were heartily glad when we, not without difficulty, induced them to land at Little Missouri, which we reached just before sunset. They were evidently disgusted because we did not take them further on their journey, and they did not show any gratitude for the service we had already rendered them. I feel sure they would have enjoyed nothing so much, if they had had the chance, as scalping our whole party.

Before leaving these redskins I may mention that I was told that certain ancient forts of great antiquity had recently been discovered near Mandan. These forts are supposed to have been built by the Mandan tribe of Indians, who have long been extinct. They are constructed most scientifically, and give evidence of a very remarkable knowledge of what are believed to be modern principles of strategic warfare, far in advance of any of our latter-day Indians. So I suppose we may take it that the race has degenerated.

CHAPTER XVI.

LITTLE MISSOURI TO THE WONDERLAND.

IT was at the railway station of Little Missouri that I had my first real experience of that rough and reckless mode of life which is inseparable from the outward margin of civilisation, where the ordinary course of law is difficult and uncertain, where everyone carries his life in his hand, and where Judge Lynch (not a bad Judge, by the way) is supreme. Little Missouri is in a basin sourrounded by hills, many of quaint shape, and looking like the partly-burnt ballast-heaps of the giants. Lignite abounds in this locality, and has been burning for ages over many square miles, reducing the strata of clay in which it is found to red fragments of brick. This imports a beautiful rose tint to the "buttes" (pronounced "butes"), and consequently a landscape sketched and coloured from nature in Pyramid Park would resemble nothing else in the world.

The "bad lands," as they are called, which lie around these parti-coloured "buttes" are not so bad as their name would imply. They are capital for grazing purposes, and among other settlers a certain French Marquis, well known in Paris, accompanied by his pretty young wife, a New York lady, has established himself. The Marquis has money and brains, and has bought much land in the locality. He has an extensive and very productive cattle "ranche," and has naturally taken up the leading position among his neighbours. He is as agreeable and handsome a man as anyone could desire to meet. It is not suprising that his success should have aroused the envy, and even jealousy, of some of his less fortunate neighbours. If matters ended here there would be no great harm done. But unfortunately men in these parts carry firearms,—and use them.

One of the first structures erected in a new settlement is a drinking saloon, where bad passions are inflamed by bad drink, and where "envy, hatred, and malice" assume a practical shape in the form of a revolver or a bowie-knife. Thus it was that the more reckless spirits among the jealous frontier men decided to finish the Marquis. But, forewarned, the Marquis turned the tables, and one of the envious cowboys (not the leader) bit the dust.

When we arrived at Little Missouri the Frenchman had just returned from a judicial investigation into the charge against him, resulting in a verdict of "justifiable homicide." He told me that his deadly foe, Frank O'Donnell, had expressed a wish to be friends for the future, and the Marquis added that he thought he was in earnest. But, for all that, neither party abated by one jot his usual precautions. Two faithful attendants, with Winchester rifles, never left the Frenchman's side, and the Marquis himself was a complete perambulating arsenal of concealed weapons.

Five minutes after speaking to him I was talking to O'Donnell, a tall, bony, not unpleasant looking man, a complete type of the frontier hunter. He was the sort of man that, if the choice were thrust upon me, I should prefer to have as a friend rather than an enemy. But if it made no difference, I should like to strike him off my visiting list altogether. He was very obliging, however, and made himself useful by bringing his influence and knowledge of their language to bear upon the Indians to induce them to quit our train. It was a strange scene, and one I shall ever remember, at that wild roadside station of Little Missouri.

I was not sorry when our engine had laid in its stock of lignite, quarried from the overhanging cliff, and delivered direct into the tender without its leaving the main line. The slouched hats, the Mexican saddles and stirrups, the leather garments, the abundant supply of weapons, added to the knowledge that a "shooting" might come off at any moment, and the station platform be strewn with corpses, not necessarily of those personally interested in the quarrel, made most of our party glad to be once more *en route*.

The train wound along among the "buttes," seeking the easiest course, and climbing up a somewhat steep gradient, until, at twenty-seven miles, the 104th degree of longitude (west of Greenwich) was passed, and we entered the territory of Montana. Thirty-nine miles more brought us to Glendive. We had now descended into the basin of the

Yellowstone River, which we were to follow to its source in the Rocky Mountains. The Yellowstone joins the Missouri near the eastern boundary of the territory at Fort Union, about sixty miles below the Glendive. Our train kept " pegging away " during the night and the whole of the next day, past Miles City (eighty miles), Big Horn (eighty-six miles), Billings (fifty-nine miles), until at five p.m. we drew up at Livingstone (115 miles). We had completed 556 miles since quitting Mandan, and were now at the entrance of the canyon, through which a further journey of sixty miles was to carry us to our destination in the great Yellowstone National Park.

There were not wanting sceptics in our party whose spirits drooped lower and lower, as day after day went by, and our train still sped on, and only boundless and monotonous prairies were in view. We breakfasted, lunched, played whist, dined, smoked, sang, recited, told tales, guessed riddles and puzzles, played cards again, went to bed, got up the next morning to find much the same scenery and no apparent progress towards our journey's end. How long would this last ? And should we be really rewarded by the wonders in "the Park?" Five days and nights had been spent in our train since leaving St. Paul, and now we had come almost suddenly upon a totally different scene. There were noble mountains with patches of snow on them, seeming in that clear atmosphere much nearer than they actually were. Here was a foretaste of something more exciting than the boundless prairie.

The "City" of Livingstone is really a village of wooden houses and shops, rising, progressing, active, and pushing. These North-West villages are all so much alike that it is difficult for the most sharp-witted tourist to distinguish between them. The National Bank is a useful test. In the eastern cities it may be a handsome structure of marble or wood; as you go West it becomes first brick, then wood, until finally it is canvas. At Livingstone it was wood.

From Livingstone a branch line diverges south from the main Northern Pacific line through the canyon, known as the Gate of the Mountains, in the direction of the Wonderland. This junction has already made Livingstone an important centre, although its existence only dates from last year. It is a rough place, and we were advised not to wander about far after dark. Our train, in which we slept, was carefully locked and guarded on its siding. The mining element is rather strong in Livingstone, and gambling saloons, with their accompanying recklessness in the matter of revolvers, are in great force.

CHAPTER XVII.

The Gate of the Mountains.

Next morning, at 5.30, after seeing a lovely sunrise from the open plain, our train plunged into the Gate of the Mountains, the sun was shut out by the lofty peaks, and I enjoyed a second, more lovely, sunrise an hour later, with all the varying lights and shadows of the snow-patched summits, which hemmed us in on all sides. A most novel and picturesque ride of three hours or more brought us to the end of the railway track. The rails were laid for a mile or two further, but for some reason or other—I think because beyond this point there was no siding or switches so as to transfer the two engines to the other end of the train, to haul it back—we were turned out here.

Some rough-looking men were seated on railway sleepers and rude benches outside a canvas drinking-saloon, the only habitation for miles.

The first piece of news that greeted us was that two hunters had just brought in a murderer, who had beaten a man's brains out with a big stone the night before. They had followed the murderer into the mountains, and there had "held him up," which means that unexpectedly—so far as he was concerned—coming upon him, with revolvers pointed at his head, they had required him to hold up his arms while they removed his weapons. I need scarcely say that had he hesitated or moved a hand in the direction of his revolver, he would have been mercilessly shot. He was now sitting quietly on a mound, talking cheerfully to one of his captors. The principal hunter, who had, so to speak, run him to earth, was a very picturesque object. His brown hair fell in long waves over his shoulders, and his handsome sunburnt face and blue eyes, naturally inspired confidence, which even his slouched hat, rough clothes, belt of cartridges, and the usual arsenal of weapons did not tend to destroy. He was well educated, spoke English like a native, was a graduate of a German university, and a most intelligent companion. I saw him frequently afterwards, and we became quite good friends. He was passing under a feigned name, and had spent five or six years amongst the "Rockies," trapping and shooting. I think his wife was dead, but he had several children living with friends in New York. Several weeks later I saw him on his way to rejoin them. He is a wonderful shot with a rifle, and is now earning his living by exhibiting his powers as a marksman in the cities further East. He told me he could with certainty hit a half dollar held between the fingers of any one endued with sufficient confidence in his powers to stand the test.

As to the murderer, he was taken to Bozeman, the chief place of the Territory, where his captors and other witnesses were held to bail to attend and prosecute him at the next assizes in December. This was in August, and the probability was that when his case came on, the prosecution would fail for lack of evidence. Not that my hunter friend meant to fail. I asked him how he intended to get over the thousands of miles from New York and back. He informed me that the Government made a liberal mileage payment to witnesses, and, as he should be able by the friendly aid of the railway authorities to travel gratis, he should make a good thing out of the trial.

No rain had fallen for weeks, and the country was brown and dusty. The prevailing vegetation consisted of a low-growing cactus spreading in all directions among the dry soil and hot stones. The temperature at daybreak had been 25 deg. Fahrenheit; by 3 p.m. the thermometer stood at 105 degs. in the shade. It was only a quarter-past nine now, but the sun had acquired terrific power, and blazed in a sky of amazing clearness when we commenced our journey of some twelve miles from the drinking saloon (the place had no name), to the Mammoth Hot Springs. I was put into the first waggon with six others and the driver, eight in all, sitting two and two, under a canvas tilt from end to end of the vehicle.

It is superfluous to say that there were no roads, only tracks, and it was easier riding where no vehicle had been before than along the beaten route. Up hill and down dale we went, jolting, bumping, thumping on hard seats, steadying bodies and nerves as best we could. The surrounding neighbourhood for miles had been laid under contribution to provide waggons and horses for our party, and we met the various teams hurrying to the drinking saloon to meet the train, each with its accompanying cloud of thick dust. It had been anticipated that our train would have taken us further on, else these vehicles would have been in readiness on our arrival.

We had neither time nor breath to admire the scenery. Our attention was largely devoted to keeping ourselves in the waggon, and extricating our feet from the loose luggage which slid backwards or forwards at the bottom of the vehicle as we ascended or descended the hills. Finally, we descended a steep pitch, which made all else seem level, and were landed breathless, but unhurt, at the rough wooden steps of a huge wooden structure, and found ourselves at the Mammoth Hot Springs Hotel, Yellowstone Park. It was half-past twelve, and more than three hours had been spent in travelling those fearful twelve miles. I felt as if I had travelled fifty!

Yellowstone Park, Wyoming Territory (for we passed the boundary of Montana during

our last torture), is in no sense of the term
what we in England understand by "a Park."
In the United States a park is any piece of
ground set apart for the public use or enjoyment. It may be only one square mile, or it
may be, as in this case, several thousand
square miles. It is mainly in Wyoming
Territory, but it really includes a narrow strip
of the adjoining territories of Montana and
Idaho. The boundaries of the park do not
describe any natural divisions. They include
a region which stretches a few miles east of
the meridian of 110 deg. west longitude, and
about the same distance west of the meridian
of 111 deg., and a few miles north of the
parallel of 45 deg., and not quite so far south
as 44 deg. north latitude. These purely
arbitrary lines contain an area fifty-five miles
in width from east to west, and sixty-five
miles in length from north to south, or about
3,575 square miles. No portion of the park is
less than 6,000 feet above the level of the sea,
while the mountain ranges rise to a level of
from 10,000 to 12,000 feet.

In 1872 the Congress of the United States
passed an Act setting apart this large tract as

K

a public park or pleasure ground, "for the benefit and enjoyment of the people." This measure is a very remarkable example of the foresight of the Americans, for it was based upon the report of a single official survey—that of Professor Hayden in 1871—made at a time when the country was almost inaccessible, and when a lack of sufficient interest in the matter might well have been excused. The park was placed under the exclusive control of the Secretary of the Interior, who may, in his discretion, grant leases for building purpose, for terms not exceeding ten years, of small parcels of ground at such places in the park as should require the erection of buildings for the accommodation of visitors. Hence the Mammoth Hot Springs Hotel, at which we now descended dusty and wayworn.

CHAPTER XVIII.

THE MAMMOTH HOT SPRINGS.

WE were confessedly a party of pioneers, and expected to have to "rough it." But I must say that our "roughing" was, even here, greatly softened by the admixture of the "smooth." The hotel at the Mammoth Hot Springs, erected by the Yellowstone Park Improvement Company, of which Mr. Rufus Hatch is president, was simply the most remarkable product of civilization in my experience. I don't think that any of us appreciated it at its true value until after we had quitted it.

A plateau of the vast formation of sulphur and magnesia, deposited by the Hot Springs, has been selected for its site. A level area of many acres surrounds it, with mountain and forest on every side, except where, far away in the valley beneath, the Gardiner River rushes along to its junction with the Yellowstone.

The hotel is throughout of wood, except the chimneys, which are of red brick. Only a third of it has been completed at present. A very picturesque structure, with gaily painted red roof and deep verandahs, capable of accommodating a couple of hundred guests. The very trees of which it is built were growing in the adjoining woods in March; the foundations were laid in June, and in August it was crowded with travellers. The rooms and corridors are very spacious, and the latter are illuminated by the electric light. There are two excellent billiard-tables, and Steinway has presented the Yellowstone Park Improvement Company with one of his finest grand pianos. I should like to have that grand piano's opinion of the journey from the end of the railway track. It had come much farther in a waggon than I had, for the railway had advanced ten miles since its arrival.

The novelty of having anything approaching civilisation in their midst, attracted all the hunters, drivers, settlers, and "cowboys" for miles round, and they congregated in the great hall of the hotel until it resembled a stage filled with the "supers" in "Fra Diavolo."

Sombrero hats, high leather boots and leggings, belts of cartridges, and revolvers abounded, especially at night. It was rather an alarming spectacle to some of the ladies, especially when they were told that Mr. Hobart, the able but impulsive manager of the hotel, had found it necessary to pitch one of these gentlemen off the verandah some days previously, and it was rumoured that a "shooting" was possible at any moment. However, "use is second nature," and we were soon all accustoned to our melo-dramatic or operatic surroundings, and should probably have accepted a little revolver practice as an ordinary incident of everyday life.

It was really a mistake to imagine that our visitors were so dangerous as they looked. Several of them were gentlemen by birth, and had received university or public school education. These were the "failures" of society, come out here to seek their fortunes amid the rough life of the frontier. I soon came to know several of the rough fellows well, and to feel quite at home with them. But there was one peculiarity which was an insuperable drawback to the pleasure of their society, and that was their habit of chewing tobacco and spitting—no, splashing great floods of yellow juice all over the place.

When the distance from the outer world was considered—we were 2,000 miles from Chicago, and 3,000 miles from any Eastern city—the accommodation at the Hot Springs was wonderful. Certainly we had not the luxurious carpets and frescoed rooms of the Fifth Avenue Hotel at New York. But we had very good and clean beds, an excellent table, the best of champagne, and plenty of Lager beer also. The beer, by the bye, did fail for one day, and the next waggon load was eagerly watched for in its progress over the hillside, and its arrival was duly cheered.

At every meal the French cook used to give us that great luxury in such a climate—American ice cream. I say "American" ice cream advisedly, for you must cross the Atlantic to taste ice cream in perfection. It is a staple article of food with them in the hot weather. *A propos* of the French cook, who was an importation from New York, having arrived only a day or two before our party, he bore the journey pretty well, until he came to the descent of the last hill before reaching the hotel, and then he exclaimed, " Do you mean to tell me that any one will come here for pleasure ?"

Facing the verandah of the hotel we saw a picturesque range of mountains, in the middle distance were wooded hills, and in the near foreground was the most remarkable object in the Park—a vast white and yellow mass, resembling nothing so much as the Rhône Glacier, but of greater dimensions, protruding from the side of the mountain. This was the more recent deposit of the Mammoth Hot Springs. By "recent" I mean since the geological period known as the glacial epoch ; for these springs were active long before that date, and the actual area of their deposits is many square miles in extent.

I devoted such spare time as I had to a careful examination of the country round this formation, and I discovered distinct traces in two instances of lofty craters which must have been active in remote ages before they were partially buried beneath the moraine which now surrounds them. Our time in the Park was far too limited for anything more than the most cursory investigation of a portion only of its natural wonders.

In the plateau on which the hotel stands are numerous extinct craters, baby geysers, small boiling lakes, and bottomless caves. The whole of the drainage of the hotel is carried into one of these extinct geysers, and it was a matter for speculation as to what effect, irritating or otherwise, it might have upon the hidden machinery and the unseen workers in the regions below!

The soil, if so it can be called, is an incrustation of brimstone, but, save for the sense of insecurity, not unpleasant to walk upon.

A lovely wood of pines, yew, and juniper, carpeted by sage brush and cactus, tempted me to wander to the blue sparkling waters of the Gardiner River. There I found several anglers. I was, unfortunately, not provided with a fishing rod, but one of our party, Mr. Thomas Mack, of Boston, had gone to the river for the express purpose of doing what has been so contemptuously discredited in England, but which is a common feat in the Park, namely, to catch a fish in one stream, and cook it immediately in another without shifting your position. The Water of the geysers is boiled at great pressure, and certainly for some reason retains its heat much longer than ordinary boiling water. A stream of this boiling water comes out of the earth and runs for some distance by the side of the Gardiner River before joining it. The Gardiner abounds with small and not very healthy trout, which are easily caught. Mr. Mack was not long in hooking a fish, and he dropped it, still hanging to the hook, into the geyser water, which, being hotter than he expected, cooked the trout so quickly that it almost fell to pieces. A second attempt was more successful, and in a few minutes a second fish was caught and cooked, several of us partaking of morsels of it, for the sake of saying that we had done so. The earlier as well as the later travellers to the Yellowstone Park have had their stories discredited. But I can assure my readers that this fish catching and cooking holds a very unimportant place among the wonderful curiosities of the region. The whole Park, or rather series of Parks, is or has been, more or less given up to this geyser action, and I can well understand how the

Indians avoided it as a place inhabited by evil spirits.

To the artist, the scene at Mammoth Hot Springs is at once an allurement and a cause of despair. Who shall give the most remote reproduction of that deep blue sky, that cloudless dome of cobalt? The hills reflect the yellows of the glorious sunshine, and at my feet is the Hot Spring Lake, a dazzling surface of brightest orange and burnt sienna. The bubbling water in the centre is of a blue, so delicately brilliant that no artificial colour could convey any idea of it.

There is but one step from the sublime to the ridiculous, and in the midst of one of nature's grandest scenes, I am compelled to compare the Hot Spring Lake to a huge cauldron, perhaps a quarter of a mile in diameter, resembling nothing so much as poaching eggs on a gigantic scale. The deepest of deep yellow yolks are there, and the whitest of froths seethe and bubble around them, while at the edge of the cauldron lies quiet clear blue water, looking so innocent, but at boiling heat.

From the terrace where I am standing, the

successive terraces of this sulphurous deposit extend for more than 1,000 feet down to the river, clothed at their base with fir, cedar, and junipers, which have thrived in the alkaline formation until they have become forest trees. Looking upward to the horizon of the mountain ridge, 2,000 feet above me, I see the same formation clothed with mighty forest trees to the summit. The terrace whereon I stand, with its giant egg-poaching establishment, is only the modern living example of the vast formation.

The ground beneath is full of rumblings and murmurings. A slight crack of a few inches wide reveals a fissure of unknown depth, from which issues a noise as of big steam-engines bubbling and hissing, while the smell I encounter beggars description. That smell of sulphuretted hydrogen pervades the park. Wherever you may go you can scarcely ever escape from it.

How dry the air is! The thermometer stands at from 90 degs. to 100 degs.—and yet the skin shows no moisture. The perspiration evaporates as quickly as it is given forth, the result being that you never feel cool. For days and weeks clouds may threaten overhead towards sunset, but there is no rain. The next morning the sky is as blue as ever.

CHAPTER XIX.

THE GEYSER BASINS.

TWENTY-SEVEN miles of hard riding or fatiguing waggon driving had to be undergone before we reached the nearest geyser basin, named, after one of the commandants of the park, the Norris Geyser Basin.

The first business was to climb the mountain side for about 3,000 feet. The road lay through a dense forest, and was the steepest, dustiest, and hottest I ever remember. After two hours' hard struggle we got our waggon and its contents safely to the plateau at the top. I did not know at the time, but I found out afterwards, that we had to return down this terrible hill. On the way back one of the waggons, team and all, turned over and tumbled down the mountain side. Fortunately the occupants had wisely taken to their feet just before the accident, and the only result was the loss of a lady's dressing bag, for the horses recovered their feet, and did not seem to trouble much about their sudden descent.

When once we were on the summit we found a long level elevated valley, with a pretty lake, called Swan Lake, but I saw no swans, for the reason that there are not any. Passing beneath the lofty cliffs of obsidian, or volcanic glass, along the shores of Beaver Lake—with obvious traces of the dams and houses of these quaint animals, all of whom have long since been trapped,—we left a poisonous green coppery stream on our right, and mounted another terrible hill chiefly of sulphur and magnesia, and catching a glimpse only of the Lake of the Woods, entered another level valley, partly prairie, partly forest, and arrived at our first night's camp at 4 p.m.

One of the greatest drawbacks of travelling in the park, is the difficulty of obtaining water that is fit to drink. On the route we had just passed there were two springs deliciously cold and pure, but all other streams, small or great, were more or less poisonous, from the coppery stream I have just mentioned, which was simply and obviously deadly, to the river by which we were now encamped, and which was highly impregnated with alkali and sulphur, although difficult to detect by the taste. When the park has been more thoroughly explored no doubt many valuable springs will be found, which will refresh the traveller of the future. About a mile from the Hot Spring Hotel there was a delicious spring very fully charged with carbonic acid gas, and which was actually an Apollinaris spring. There is much of this gas escaping on all sides, but it generally finds its way to the open air through a hot medicated water. No doubt this Apollinaris spring will yet be turned to profitable account, with many other valuable Brünnen at present unknown.

Our camp made a good deal of show externally, but it was not well provided. The ravenous tourist was difficult to satisfy. Our cook and his wife lost their tempers and their civility. The accommodation was not equal to the demand, and I was not sorry, when darkness closed round us, to wrap myself in a rough grey blanket, put my overcoat under my head for a pillow, and sleep on the bare ground the sleep of the just.

The Norris Geyser Basin was about half-a-mile beyond our camp, and was on our route to the Lower Geyser, Midway Geyser, and Upper Geyser Basins, the first of which is about twenty and the last about thirty miles distant. The Norris Geyser Basin is doubtless the oldest and the highest in the Park, being about 7,400 feet above sea level. Its geysers are not so large as some at the Upper Basin, notably those known as "Old Faithful," "The Castle," "The Giant," "The Giantess," "The Beehive," and others. But the Norris Basin has this great advantage over the others, that it is the first "fire-hole" that greets the astonished eyes of the visitor who enters the park from the Mammoth Hot Spring side. It is of vast extent, and jets of steam rise from the white surface as far as the eye can reach up to the low fir-clad hills that are its boundary.

Beyond, in the extreme distance, rise the bare, parched mountains of the Gallatin Range. The whole basin is a collection of hot springs and pools, varying greatly in colour. "Frying-pans," as the guides call them, sputter and hiss violently; "paint-pots" boil and bubble; and geysers, little and big, throw up their columns of water at long or short intervals. The earth rumbles and shakes, and the air is hot and stinks abominably. Where the water does not boil over, it seethes and gurgles underneath, and great caution is necessary in selecting your path where the surface is so treacherous.

The chief geyser in this basin is known as "The Monarch." He is said to spout once in twenty-four hours, throwing up an immense volume of boiling water through three capacious orifices to a height of over one hundred feet. The eruption lasts for about twenty minutes. When I was there, of course it was not his time for showing off his powers, but he was very busy getting ready his forces for another display. We did our best to provoke him, by pitching great lumps of rock down his throat so as to destroy the equilibrium below. But he contented himself with grumbling severely for a short time, and then returned to his normal condition of active preparation. However, there were plenty of less important geysers to exhibit the working of the machinery. There is a most useful little model geyser called the "Minute Man," which punctually once every sixty seconds spouts a bold stream to the height of twenty-five feet or thirty feet from an orifice about six inches in diameter. I should add that "The Monarch" had cleared the ground for his operations by blowing out a large gap in the side of the mountain.

Surrounded by fir trees whitened by the steam and spray, is "The Workshop," and certainly it is well named, for the varied sounds given forth by this "fumarole" exactly resemble the noise of a busy establishment with much machinery hard at work. In fact it is difficult to believe that there is not some place of the kind among the trees. Another very striking effect is produced by a "blow-hole" in the rocks by the side of the road. The name of "The Steamboat Vent" has been given to this evident safety valve. You feel instinctively that if the safety valve were screwed down, the appalling force of the steam must necessarily lift the neighbourhood far and near into the air. The steam escaping from "The Steamboat Vent" is so superheated, that it is not visible in the form of steam for some distance after it leaves the ground. Its roar is awful, and branches of trees laid across the aperture shrivel up in a few moments.

In these various basins, besides many others less important, the apertures whence steam, water, or coloured mud are discharged have never been counted. I should say there must be hundreds, if not thousands. Some geysers discharge their contents in such a manner that a deposit is formed round the aperture, which assumes in many instances fantastic shapes. Thus you have the Monument, the Castle, the Beehive, the Orange, the Liberty Cap (an extinct geyser), &c.

"Old Faithful" in the Upper Basin is the tourist's pet geyser, because of the frequency and regularity with which his magnificent eruptions occur, thus affording excellent opportunities for observation. Its crater, an oblong opening, two feet by six feet, is situated on a mound of geyserite about twelve feet in height. This mound is composed of layers of deposit formed in the manner referred to above. "Old Faithful" "operates," as the Americans say, every hour or thereabouts, throwing a large column of water for four or five minutes to a height of 100 feet or 150 feet. This geyser affords amusement to the tourist by kindly acting as a laundry on occasion. Pocket-handkerchiefs placed in the crater during the period of quiescence are punctually restored, thoroughly washed, to their owners when the eruption takes place. I was told that it was made to take in washing on a larger scale sometimes, by the surveying expeditions which have camped for a long time in the Park. General Sheridan's men, in 1882, found that linen and cotton fabrics were uninjured by the action of the water, but woollen clothes were torn to shreds. The whole scene is very wonderful, very unlike anything else, very well worth seeing, extremely uncanny, and very difficult to get at. And no one can say it does not repay him.

A third hard ride brings the traveller to the climax of his journey, after which all are agreed that the majesty and beauty of the scenery of the Rockies can no farther go. It ends in the Falls of the Yellowstone River and the Grand Canyon. The Upper and Lower Falls are about half-a-mile apart. The Upper is not so grand as the Lower, but it is more picturesque. The clear height of the Fall has been accurately measured, and is 112 feet. The Lower Fall is about 310 feet in height. After quitting the pool at the foot of the Upper Fall the river turns somewhat abruptly to the left, rushing through Cascade Creek until its sea-green water leaps from the brink of the Great Fall into the Grand Canyon.

The Grand Canyon is supposed to be unique and one of the wonders of scenery. It is of the nature of a Swiss defile, and yet so totally different that the recollection of any well known pass in no way helps the description. But try to imagine a huge mountain, with two jagged summits and a " col " of the brightest coloured rock—no dull greys of slate or granite, but yellow and orange tinted strata, to which the rocks at Alum Bay may be compared as pigmies to giants; and then imagine this bright coloured mountain cloven in two to its very base, and in the fissure, flowing at an immense depth, sometimes visible, sometimes quite hidden, the Yellowstone River. It is a scene never to be forgotten.

A bridle-path goes for ten miles on the summit of the fissure on the left bank of the river. Above the path rise lofty "dents" and "aiguilles." On the opposite side are displayed the dazzling sides of the huge mountain, on which the brightest hues alternate with each other, from the most brilliant canary, orange, and bronze, to the mossy green of the river's bed. The burning rays of the sun play on these colours, shining in full force down the gully. This gorgeous scene lasts throughout a ride of ten miles, leaving an impression that can never be effaced. "Of its kind," said one of our party who gave me this description, "there is assuredly nothing finer in the whole world!"

Several of our party found their way back over Mount Washburn to the Mammoth Hot Springs Hotel, but the inadequacy of the means of transport, the want of horses, and the general breakdown of the commissariat department, added to the illness of more than one, interfered greatly with the plans as originally projected. Another summer matters will be very different and much better arranged. As it was, the majority of us retraced our steps. At one place on the road back the crust in the vicinity of a crater gave way, and the contents of one of the waggons were precipitated into it. The occupants of the vehicle, among whom were two ladies, had fortunately got out a few minutes before, otherwise the accident might have been more serious than the laughter which it aroused. Among the articles turned out into the geyser was a basket containing fresh eggs, and the negro servants from the railway train, who had accompanied us, grinned with delight when they finally fished out the eggs and found they were boiled hard!

The Great Yellowstone Lake in the south-eastern quarter of the Park was not included in our hurried tour. In itself alone are the materials to occupy the explorer for a much longer period than we had at our disposal. Up to the present it is known only to much more hardy travellers than we were. No attempt even has been made to accomodate travellers, and the hut of a trapper here or there is all the shelter its banks afford. The lake is reported to be full of curiosities, sub-aqueous boiling springs, geysers like cauldrons on its shores, and the enterprising but cautious traveller can take a hot or cold bath in its waters, as he may prefer. Strange to say, it abounds with trout, but they are unhealthy and "wormy."

The Park generally has but little game. I saw a dead bear, a tame elk, and an abundance of wild ducks. Possibly the bears, buffalo, elk, and other large game go elsewhere during the summer months. Elk is plentiful somewhere in the vicinity, because we had it as food at the hotel. But the sportsman—and we had a good many in our party—will assuredly be disappointed if he goes to the Yellowstone Park in the hope of securing a great bag. Our sporting friends had gone prepared to find bears and wolves as plentiful as blackberries, and were provided with such an arsenal of weapons and ammunition as to be objects of apprehension to their more peaceful fellow-travellers. But they never killed anything or (happily) anybody. One of the party went away with a hunter into the mountains for ten days, but he only killed one elk and some ducks, catching, however, an abundance of fine trout.

In addition to the wrong impression which has gone abroad with regard to the abundance of game, there is another very prevalent in the United States, and that is that there are glaciers among the mountains. As an old and very unworthy member of the Alpine Club, I may be allowed, at any rate, to say that I know a glacier when I see one. In this part of the range of the Rocky Mountains, I saw some detached patches of snow remaining unmelted from last winter and lodged in deep hollows and crevices. But there was not a trace of a glacier. The limit of perpetual snow in Switzerland is about 9,500 feet. The mountains of the Yellowstone rise to 10,000 feet or 12,000 feet, and the Park is considerably south of Switzerland, and in a country under very different climatic conditions. There is an abundance of beauty and interest in the Yellowstone Park, but it is not, and never can be, a Switzerland.

The roads, which are now unworthy of the name, are being rapidly improved by the

United States Government. President Arthur, accompanied by General Sheridan, Mr. Secretary Lincoln, Mr. Crosby, Governor of Montana, Captain Clark, and others made the tour of the Park this season, with mounted military escort, baggage mules, and relays of horses. Even with so many advantages the task was not an easy one. There are difficulties of climate, the sulphurous soil and smells, the heat, and the sometimes sudden changes of temperature to frost at night. Moreover, the supply of water has to be chosen with great care, or the traveller may be prostrated. Warnings are to be put up at the poisonous springs, rivers, and lakes, and notice given also to travellers when they may freely drink of the roadside springs, or bathe in wholesome water. The uncertainty of procuring fresh food, wine, or spirits, makes it advisable for each party to provide themselves to a great extent with their own supplies, and not to depend upon the chance of what they may find at the "Hotel Tents" in the interior. The supply of horses, too, is at present quite inadequate to the demand of the travellers, when their numbers, the badness of the paths, and the length of the stages—twenty, thirty, or forty miles—are considered. But we, pioneers, cheerfully submitted to these disadvantages, feeling that the energetic Americans will have many improvements by next summer and in every succeeding summer.

So new is the Yellowstone Park to the people in the Eastern States of the Union, that no photographs of its geysers could be obtained in New York, when we were there. But the State Department at Washington is causing large maps, drawings, and photographs to be made. Their *employés* were engaged on this work last summer, and any art publisher can now be furnished with copies on application. Dr. Oskar Berggruen, of Vienna, who was one of my companions, is about to reproduce them in his forthcoming book on the Yellowstone Park, which will be translated into French and English, and will be one of the most valuable additions to the literature of the Yellowstone yet given to the public.

On the return journey to the Hot Springs Hotel we suffered terribly from heat, especially when, on the open prairie near Swan Lake, where there was not a particle of shade, our team, which had been a great trouble and anxiety to us all day, finally gave out. One of our horses fell as if dying, and the other declined to struggle on any farther. The heat was awful. Our driver, a particularly pleasant young fellow, appealed, and happily not in vain, to a "freighter," who was ahead of us with two waggons and two teams, to spare us one team. With that desire to help one another in difficulty, which is a marked characteristic of the rough denizens of the frontier, this man immediately hitched one of his waggons on behind the other, and taking the team thus set at liberty put the horses to our waggon and drove us to the end of our journey down the terrible hill, which I have already described.

We found Judge Pierrepoint quitting his carriage in order to make this dangerous descent, which he thought it safer to do on foot. The Judge, who was formerly American Minister in London, had been furnished with mules and a military escort by the United States Government, and was travelling, so to speak, in grand style. I had afterwards, the pleasure of having him as my partner in many a friendly rubber of whist, during our stay at the Mammoth Hot Springs Hotel, and a very good "hand" he played. In America they have a species of whist which is neither "long" nor "short," but between the two. Seven points are "game," and "honours" are not counted.

Several days passed before the whole of our scattered party was once more collected under the roof of the Hot Springs Hotel. It was a happy result when all had got back without injury beyond that arising from heat, bad food and water, and fatigue. Each detachment as it arrived had its own special story of difficulty, danger, or disappointment. The negro servants shook their heads earnestly, and told me they did not like it at all. But, then, who expected that they would? For myself, I suffered up to the time I left the district from a mild but unpleasant attack of fever of an intermittent character.

One day the President of the United States arrived with all his party at the superintendent's house, the most conspicuous object on the mound in front of the hotel. It gave us a new sensation to see the "Stars and Stripes" flying like the Royal Standard to inform our small world that the Head of the State was in our neighbourhood.

After dinner that evening we went in a body to serenade the President, who received us by his camp fire. It was a sight never to be forgotten, so wild and so strange was it. Later in the evening President Arthur returned our visit, bringing with him General Sheridan, Secretary Lincoln, and the other members of his party. We were all especially interested in making the acquaintance of General Sheridan, who is not only a remarkable man, but a remarkable looking man, being very short and stout, in fact, almost as broad as he is long. He has grown much stouter since the time when he made his celebrated "Ride" of twenty miles to the fight.

I was especially favoured by being placed on the President's right hand when we adjourned for a cigar to a private room. I found him a most courteous and agreeable man, ready to speak of public matters with less reserve than I should have anticipated. He had much to tell me of his travels in Alaska and Oregon. He was also good enough to give me his views on Ireland, Protection, and Fair Trade. I found from him that his grandfather had fought at Waterloo, and that he still preserved as a valued heirloom a decoration which had been bestowed upon his ancestor by the Duke of Kent.

The President and I had both been "roughing it," but he had undergone much more of it than I had. We had both been out of the vicinity of washerwomen for some weeks; but I flattered myself that he looked the shabbier and dirtier of the two as we sat side by side; besides, the skin hung in strips on his nose, which did not improve his appearance.

However, I enjoyed a very pleasant chat with him for three-quarters of an hour, and I doubt if any other Englishman ever before had an interview under similar circumstances with any of the chiefs of the Great Republic across the Atlantic.

The next morning, soon after sunrise, he broke up his camp, and, making for the nearest point of the railway, returned to Washington.

CHAPTER XX.

Sitting Bull at Bismarck.

On the morning of my departure from the Mammoth Hot Springs Hotel, I was awakened at an early hour by the sounds of the "Steinway." It was a well-known popular tune which reminded me strongly of home.

A family of Americans, travelling, as is their habit, with all their children, had arrived a few days before. The ladies remained at the hotel, while the gentlemen made the tour of the Park. One of the girls, with a sweet voice, had taken possession of the "Steinway," and was singing "In the gloaming," which was soon followed by some selections from "Patience." Later, Mr. Hermann, of New York, who was one of our party, favoured us with a succession of magnificent performances, bringing out all the brilliant qualities of the piano. Mr. Hermann's taste and execution are well known, and as a pianist he is unsurpassed. The music seemed somehow to match the glorious sunshine outside.

Anything more beautiful than that morning it is impossible for the most lively imagination to picture. The sun blazed from a cloudless sky of the richest blue A light cool air fanned our cheeks. The atmosphere was so free from any trace of mist or haze that, without exaggeration, mountains twenty miles away seemed within an easy stroll. Our drive to the termination of the railway was one prolonged chorus of amazement and delight.

During our stay in the Park the line had been advanced seven miles, which very materially reduced our rough waggon-ride. The Negro bed-boy of our car, a most civil, pleasant fellow, grinned unmistakable delight at our return, and we were not less pleased to see him, and to be once more in our travelling hotel, the railway train. The ride back by the red-coloured rocks of the Cinnabar Mountain and the Devil's Slide, and so through the Gate of the Mountains to Livingstone, was very lovely, its grandeur being heightened by

M

the gathering thunderclouds over the lofty peaks. No rain fell, however, and after an hour's delay our train started on its long Eastward return journey along the Northern Pacific line.

Our numbers were somewhat reduced, for several of our party had left us for sporting purposes, and others had gone further west to the Pacific Coast, intending to visit San Francisco, and return by Utah and the Salt Lake. During the next night others parted from us to visit a large "ranche" belonging to one of our companions, a most agreeable gentleman from St. Louis. This disintegrating process continued as we went eastward, until we arrived at New York a mere remnant of the seventy who had inaugurated the Hot Springs Hotel three weeks before.

All through the night our train sped steadily along, and without any incident worthy of record, until late the next afternoon we were landed at Mandan, where we were to remain all night, crossing the Missouri the following morning in order to be present at the laying of the foundation stone of the Capitol at Bismarck. Here we were to meet the large party invited by Mr. Villard, the—I regret to say—late president of the Northern Pacific Railroad. Monetary difficulties have necessitated his resignation. But I am anticipating. At Mandan we found, in the large room of the railway station, no less a person than the great Chief of the Sioux Indians, Sitting Bull, the warrior who has earned the modified respect of the Americans by having dared to declare war against the United States!

Although only sixty miles from the "agency" where he is bound to reside, he was regarded with interest as a curiosity by the Americans themselves, as well as by the foreigners of our party.

Sitting Bull was accompanied by his sister, Beautiful Feather, and his cousin, the wife of Spotted Horn Bull, and by Gray Eagle, Bone Tomahawk, Fool Heart, Tall-as-the-Cloud, Crow Eagle, Horn Bull, Two Bears, Long Soldier, Long Dog, and Holy Ghost. The origin of the last name I was quite unable to discover. These notabilities were attended by the captain, sergeant, and four soldiers of the Indian police, all in Uncle Sam's uniform, and apparently very proud of the distinction.

They were also accompanied by Major M'Laughlin and his wife from the agency. The dress of the Indians consisted for the most part of an army blanket, buckskin leggings, a necklace of beads or teeth, and the regulation bad beaver hat, punched in many places, and ornamented with turkey tail feathers. Sitting Bull himself had no hat, but from the scalp, which, as an American bystander remarked, he has worn too long, protruded a pair of eagle's feathers. Sitting there, surrounded by his brother savages, looking more like an old woman than a chief, wrinkled, silent, dirty, he was a most objectionable looking person.

Now and then he exchanged some guttural remark with his neighbours, while all the time he was busy driving bargains for his signature at the rate of 1 dollar 50 cents. each. Most of my companions were good customers to him, not only for his signature, but for beads, necklaces, bracelets, and any article he had to spare. For my part I had no desire to touch, much less possess, anything belonging to him. His eyes glanced furtively around as if he might be suspecting treachery. Occasionally what seemed to be a smile passed over his hideous countenance, but the effect produced was, as the bystander before alluded to remarked, about as attractive as a stray bit of sunshine upon a heap of mud, His intelligence is no doubt vastly superior to that of his fellows, but that is not saying much.

It is alleged that he has but to raise his finger to provoke a fresh war between the races. I very much question whether the finger will be raised; but there is no knowing. On this point, and on other matters connected with the Indians, there is no better authority than Father Stephan, the Roman Catholic priest of Fargo. Father Stephan is now between sixty-five and seventy years of age, with white hair and beard, tall and erect, and with a prepossessing expression of face. Educated in the Ecole Polytechnique of Belgium, he has been in turn civil engineer, soldier, priest, Government agent, and missionary. He believed when I saw him, that he had converted Sitting Bull and his sister to Christianity, and they were to be baptised into the Roman Catholic Church at an early date. The miserable Pagan, however, declined to be baptised, and join the Church when he found that it would conflict with his polygamous tastes. He refused point blank to give up either of his squaws, and his baptism is consequently indefinitely postponed.

Father Stephan does not think that the Sioux—pronounced "Soos"—surrendered all their arms and ammunition. He believes they have a large store of rifles cached at the present moment and, while they may never again be used, except in the hunt, it is neither the policy nor the nature of the Indian to part with them or to reveal their place of concealment. As to the final solution of the Indian problem, it is Father Stephan's opinion that the Sioux Indian is shrewd enough to see that he can no longer successfully compete with the white man; that the country is filling, and he is being practically surrounded by a race of brave and hardy settlers, that towns and villages are springing up around his reservations, railroads running to their very edge and waiting to get in, and that under these circumstances he must either remain quiet, or yield to force.

"Treat these men," said Father Stephan,

"fairly and honestly, and they will make good citizens; if not, there will be trouble in the future."

I suggested that the Government did not act wisely in encouraging the distinction of race, and keeping the Indians in idleness as pensioners of the State. Would it not be better for both parties if habits of industry were encouraged, and the Indians taught to fight the battle of life side by side with the citizens? They would thus become interested in the general welfare of the nation, and be gradually absorbed. To this I got no definite reply.

The next morning at sunrise we crossed that superb specimen of engineering, the steel railway bridge over the Missouri, and arrived at Bismarck. It was now about seven o'clock, and the streets near the railway station were filled with people, horses, and vehicles. Finding I had a quarter of an hour to spare, I was rash enough to place myself in the hands of a local barber. The crowds, the bands of music, the Indians, and all the life of the streets distracted the attention of my "operator," so that, while professing utter indiff-

erence to the procession and ceremonies, he
held on to my nose with one hand, his razor
flashed in the other, while one eye was on my
chin and the other looked out of the window.
It was a very bad quarter of an hour so far
as I was concerned.

About half-past seven a procession was
formed and went to the site of the Capitol,
three-quarters of a mile north of the town, on
the hill. There were firemen, volunteers,
bands, citizens, and guests in carriages, ladies,
gentlemen, and small boys on horseback, and
an immense throng of people of all classes
and conditions on foot, all hurrying as fast as
they could across the prairie. A waggon-load
of little girls dressed in white attracted my
attention, for they looked at a distance like a
Sunday school in a van, but on a nearer view
I saw they represented little gods and
goddesses of various sorts. Of course the
Goddess of Liberty was not left unrepresented,
but she had a car to herself, and was a full-
grown woman. Hard work she had, too, to
preserve her equilibrium in her rapid jolt
across the fields.

The Indians had got themselves up in a

fresh coat of red paint, and looked very flushed and comical with their rubble-stained cheeks. Sitting Bull had daintily tipped the eagle's feathers on his head with red ribbon. On the line of route I crossed an unenclosed plot of ground which was obviously an old burial-ground. I was told that most of those interred there had "died with their boots on;" in other words had come to some sudden and violent end in the rough, gambling, lawless days of the past.

Of course there were banners of all sorts and sizes, covered with emblems, portraits of the German Chancellor, and mottoes. "Welcome to Henry Villard," "Welcome to Rufus Hatch," "Welcome to Sitting Bull," "Welcome to Everybody to Dakota, the Eden of the World."

One banner especially amused me. It was carried by a singularly stolid-looking young man, who seemed thoroughly bored by the whole proceeding. Over the banner, attached to the pole, were gilded models of agricultural implements, sickle, scythe, rake, plough, &c., while on the silk suspended underneath was a rather well painted chubby goddess of Agriculture, and below in clear gilt characters, "In his signibus vinces." Possibly Dakota may intend to start a Latin of its own. But perhaps I ought to have been satisfied at finding the classics recognised at all so far West, and should not have criticised Dakota's adaptation of the well known motto too severely.

After the first stone had been duly laid, and General Grant had spoken the longest speech he was ever known to make, followed by the "orating" of other notabilities, another hurry-scurry across the prairie landed us again at the railway station. Here we exchanged hearty greetings with a number of English friends, who were going West in the Villard trains, for there were several—the party being so large that no single train could possibly contain it. The "Villards" went one way in detachments, and the "Hatches" went the other, in a compact body, at noon.

As night came on, the effect produced by the burning of the straw on the great farms was singularly impressive. At present the only way of disposing of the straw after the grain is threshed out is to burn it. This is terribly wasteful, but doubtless a more profitable method of dealing with it will come in time. The burning of these thousands of tons of straw illuminates the country for miles round, and when first seen is certainly rather alarming.

We reached Fargo at eleven o'clock, but only remained a short time to look at the decorations of the station, which had been left untouched for our especial benefit. At noon the next day we were at St. Paul, and in about twenty-six hours more we reached Chicago, where we rested for a few days and enjoyed the hospitality and kind attentions of some of our companions whose homes were in Chicago.

The word "home" reminds me of the pretty way in which Americans use the expression. In England we say, "Come to my house." In America they say, "Come and see me at my home." I did so, and shall always remember the hospitable welcome I received.

CHAPTER XXI.

Back to New York.—Washington.

No one should miss the opportunity of travelling between Chicago and New York by the Pennsylvania Railroad. There is no finer example of railway construction and management than that portion of the line between Pittsburgh and New York, a run of 444 miles, which is made with but three stoppages—at Altoona (117 miles), at Harrisburg (132 miles), and at Philadelphia (105 miles). The Limited Express accomplishes the entire distance between Chicago and New York, over 1,000 miles, in twenty-six-and-a-half hours, regardless of the steep gradients encountered in crossing the Alleghany Mountains. Throughout its entire length the line is laid with a double track of steel rails fastened to oak sleepers embedded in broken stone ballast, with splice joints between the sleepers (which are apparently not more than six inches or eight inches apart), so arranged that the connection on one side comes opposite to the centre of the rail on the other, thus preventing the jar which is often so uncomfortable with the ordinary method of construction. It is certainly the steadiest line I ever travelled upon. The engine takes up its water supply from the track tanks as it goes along, and the time is made by uniformity of progress more than by increased speed.

The scenery of the Alleghany Mountains is very fine. They are, however, gigantic hills rather than mountains, clothed with dense forests to their rounded tops, and separated by valleys miles in width. At the summit the train passes through a tunnel 2,160 feet above sea level, and 1,200 yards in length. Just before reaching this point, Cresson Springs, a favourite summer resort is passed, but so rapidly that there is only time to glance at the gigantic wooden hotel known as "Mountain House," where 1,000 guests can be comfortably accommodated. After quitting the tunnel we get our first view of Altoona, far away, where the extensive workshops of the railway company are situated, and which is now a town of 20,000 inhabitants. At Kittatinny Point the road is carried round a curve which is one of the wonders of engineering. This is the famous Horse Shoe Bend. The traveller ought to be careful so to arrange his journey that he may traverse this portion of the line by daylight. The difference in time between Chicago and New York is about an hour, so that, travelling eastward, everything happens before you expect it, and your watch is worse than useless.

I had no actual experience of a journey by this celebrated Limited Express train, which leaves Chicago at 5 p.m. and arrives in New York the following evening at 7.25. Our party was still too large, although greatly reduced in numbers, to be accommodated on a train of this character. So we had to leave by the mail forty minutes later, arriving in New York eleven hours after the Express. This gave us two nights in the cars, from Monday afternoon to Wednesday morning.

So ended our long picnic into the Great North-West, a journey which I shall always look back upon with extreme pleasure. It gave me the opportunity of becoming acquainted with a number of the most agreeable Americans from all parts of the States, and of appreciating their many good qualities, among which a warm-hearted hospitality is not the least. Many of them are almost more English than we are ourselves, occupying now the same homesteads in which their ancestors have lived uninterruptedly for 250 years. Traces of old English manners and customs still survive among them which have long been lost to us. There is, in short, so much to bind together the two great branches of the Anglo-Saxon race on either side of the Atlantic that it ought to be our interest, as I am sure it would be our pleasure, to promote this union.

Having some days to spare before the departure of the *Britannic* for Liverpool, we determined to utilise them by paying a visit to Philadelphia, Baltimore, and Washington. The distance from New York to Washington is 260 miles, and is accomplished with few stoppages in six hours. The change from New York to a point so many miles due south produces a marked difference in the temperature, which is apparent everywhere.

I had hitherto only noticed stray patches of tobacco plants, but, as we traversed Maryland, tobacco was to be seen growing in large fields, while considerable tracts were covered with tomatoes. The first view of the Capitol at Washington is very impressive, its white dome being visible for many miles. The railway enters the city along the middle of the street, with houses, footways, and carriage ways on each side. It seemed as if every person we saw in the streets and at the doors of the houses was either a negro or more or less coloured. This was because we were traversing the poorer portion of the town, for the white population actually outnumbers the coloured in the proportion of two to one. The train eventually came to a stand in the very grounds attached to the Capitol, for shrubs, flower-beds, broad walks, and green grass plots extended up to the base of the great white building.

The Baltimore and Potomac River Railway Depôt at which I had arrived, was the scene of the assassination of President Garfield. A marble tablet in the wall of the waiting-room records the fact, while a brass star let into the floor marks the exact spot.

It was certainly warm at Washington. Let there be no mistake about that. And there were mosquitoes, strong able-bodied creatures, anxious to make the acquaintance of the succulent stranger! Never having been troubled by them during the whole of my journey, I was unprepared for their attack, and many were the apologies at my hotel for the oversight in not providing me with mosquito curtains, when it was too late, and had become a question whether I should not have erysipelas. A friendly negro waiter, who fanned me as I ate my breakfast, said, " very strange, sir, but they never bite me!" " No," I replied, not wishing to retort harshly, " but you see they like to eat of a fresh dish."

How hot it was that Sunday morning as we slowly made our way on foot to the Episcopal Church of the Holy Cross at the corner of Massachusetts Avenue and Eighteenth Street. I chanced, in making some enquiries, to address myself to the Rector's wife, who entered most pleasantly into conversation, and begged us not to go away after service without speaking to her husband, the Rev. Dr. Harrold.

The Church of the Holy Cross occupies a lovely situation on high ground, standing on a plot which is unenclosed, a triangular space covered with grass, and with frontage on three roads. The building is simple and unpretending, of brick, painted a dull olive green. After service Dr. Harrold told me of his struggles and difficulties, on which point Mrs. Harrold had already enlightened me. He had fought his way bravely, and I hope he may long live to enjoy the more prosperous state which now seems in store for him.

Fifteen years ago he bought the plot on which the Church stands for 500 dollars. It was then far outside the city, but latterly the building of handsome residences had extended up to and beyond it. The land had increased amazingly in value. He had just been offered 40,000 dollars for it, and had made up his mind that he would accept 50,000 dollars, which would enable him to buy a cheaper plot elsewhere and transfer his church to it, besides leaving a sum sufficient for a moderate endowment.

The service was conducted entirely by himself, his family assisting him in the choir and at the organ. It was a very earnest hearty service, possibly too Ritualistic to please every-one, but the Rector had decided opinions of his own, and had gathered round him a good body of supporters of whom he was justly proud. I shall never forget his sermon. It was the Sunday following Holy Cross Day, the festival of the dedication of the church, and he made that the subject of his discourse. One passage was very characteristic. He was describing the manner in which he had freed the church from debt, an operation which he had accomplished, although, as he said, " we have never had a fair, we have never had a dance, we have never had a frolic, we have never had a candy-pull, we have never had a molasses stew!" I had neither the time nor the courage to ask him to explain to me more in detail these various methods of obtaining money for church purposes, and also whether he had said " stew " or " chew," of which I am uncertain.

I must not forget to mention that nearly every person in the congregation had a fan.

The women fanned themselves, the men fanned themselves, and the organ blower worked the bellows with one hand, while with the other he performed the double duty of fanning himself and the organist.

CHAPTER XXII.

WASHINGTON—PHILADELPHIA.

ARLINGTON House, on Arlington Heights, about four miles from the Capitol, formerly the home of Washington's adopted son, and afterwards the residence of the celebrated Confederate General Robert E. Lee, who married a daughter of that adopted son, is well worthy of a visit. The surrounding park and gardens, with their grand old forest trees, are essentially English, and the house itself is an interesting but ugly old English house of the last century, with heavy stucco pillars and portico. In fact, were it not for the lovely view of the Potomac and the brilliantly white Capitol in the distance I could have believed I was in England. The house is entirely denuded of furniture, except a desk for the visitors' book, a friendly dog or two, and a grumpy custodian who had lost his arm (and his temper) at Gettysburg.

In 1864 General Lee's estate at Arlington Heights was confiscated by a special Bill in Congress, and was sold by the Government, except 200 acres which were set apart as a national cemetery. In this cemetery lie the bodies of 16,000 soldiers who fell in the war of Secession. A vast number have neat graves and headstones, and the unknown, to the number of 2,111, whose bones were gathered from the battlefields of Bull Run, and the route to the Rappahannock after the war, are mingled in one common grave, over which is placed a granite sarcophagus.

The bitter feelings naturally engendered by the war have to a great extent become things of the past and the value of the, estate was afterwards restored by Congress to General Lee's heirs. So also with other matters. There was a time when no Federal regiment ever passed through Harper's Ferry, the scene of Captain John Brown's insurrection in 1859, and practically the starting point of the war, without singing the well known chant,

"John Brown's body lies rotting in the grave,
But his soul goes marching on."

Now all is changed, and the only experience

I had of the great anti-slavery monomaniac was a curious fact in his family history recorded in a modified version of the old war song, and sung by American and British members of the Rufus Hatch party during their last evening together on the cars between Chicago and New York—viz.,

"John Brown's baby had a pimple on its nose!"

The Londoner has become accustomed to see the Virginian Creeper, or *Ampelopsis hederacea*, as I believe the botanists call it, flourishing luxuriantly all over the metropolis. It has taken kindly to the London atmosphere and is valued by us all in proportion. Naturally, being in Virginia, I looked for my old friend, expecting to see its luxuriance increased tenfold in that lovely climate. Not at all. The contrary effect is produced. In London the vigour of the plant is expended in putting forth endless trailing shoots and masses of foliage, with occasional bunches of a stunted insignificant flower. In Virginia, on the other hand, its efforts take another direction, and, in some examples which I saw, the rich purple berries, hanging in clusters, were more conspicuous and abundant than the leaves.

I had vowed solemnly, on going to America, that I would not leave the country without seeing the original Declaration of Independence, and more especially the original draft of the same, in Jefferson's handwriting, corrected and toned down a little by Adams. Jefferson was so proud of having done this, that he wished for nothing else to be recorded upon his tomb except the fact that he wrote the original Declaration of Independence. Now, as a foreigner—not that I could ever be convinced that I was a foreigner,—I naturally expected that these two original documents would be most carefully treasured, and their whereabouts known to every American. They were, in fact, so carefully treasured that no one seemed to know where they were!

The first rebuff I received in my search at Washington was from one of the most distinguished members of the United States Bar, who said he believed they were in Philadelphia. Not disheartened, I asked at the Capitol, and was referred to the Patent Office, where I had the satisfaction of being shown the place where they had formerly been. The official in the room was not quite sure whether they had been returned to Philadelphia or were in the National Museum. I determined to try the Museum, in spite of the heat, and the fact that everything in Washington is a mile at least from everything else. It has been rightly named the "City of Magnificent Distances."

The National Museum received me with courtesy, but the object of my quest was not there. The "Washington relics" were there, and I was urged to step inside and inspect them, but I was not to be diverted from my purpose at that time. I was recommended to try the Smithsonian Institution, which adjoins the Museum, as a likely place to find the Declaration. I did so, but with no result, excepting that I had the advantage of seeing a most picturesque Gothic building of red sandstone, erected at a cost of £90,000, with money bequeathed to the United States by an Englishman, James Smithson, a natural son of the first Duke of Northumberland. The official who received me assured me that the Declaration really was in the National Museum, although the authorities seemed not to be aware of it. I returned to the Museum and enjoyed an inspection of the "Washington relics," which are most interesting, and are all nicely arranged and preserved in glass cases. But there was no "Declaration of Independence!"

Somebody now suggested that the Declaration might possibly be in the State Department just beyond the White House. If it were not there, it was impossible to say where it could be found. At this moment, almost in a state of dissolution from the intense heat, I saw for the first, and almost the only time in America, a hansom cab. In another minute I was seated in it.

The pavements of Washington are excellent, being mainly of asphalte, and my hansom rolled smoothly along. What bliss! and the cost not excessive; 75 cents., or 3s. an hour.

At the State Department my perseverance was rewarded by a sight of the documents of which I was in search. There they were, carefully framed behind plate glass in a folding mahogany frame, so that both sides could be inspected. The Declaration itself is nearly illegible from having had a press *facsimile* taken of it, so that the signatures are almost obliterated, but the original draft by

Jefferson is perfect. The courteous official who accompanied me was evidently much amused by the interest I took in the documents, and the personal discomfort which their thorough inspection necessitated, for they are fixed at such a low level that I had to kneel on the hard tiled floor in order to see them properly.

I called at the White House, hoping to have the honour of renewing my acquaintance with President Arthur under more civilised conditions than those under which we met in the Wonderland of the Rocky Mountains. Unfortunately he had gone to New York to attend the funeral of an old friend, but the negro hall porter who took my card showed extraordinary interest when I explained where I had met the President. That evening a military band performed a well-selected programme on the grassy slopes under the fine trees in front of the Presidential residence. The music, the electric light, the fountains, the bright moon, the orderly crowd, combined to produce a charming effect, which was only dissipated by the last piece—" Yankee Doodle "—a vulgar production unworthy of a great nation—which, however, seemed to please the sovereign people, for they insisted on an *encore*.

The visitor to the different public buildings at Washington (or Philadelphia), is assailed on every side by portraits of the General of that name in every shade of badness. There are scarcely any worth looking at as even moderate works of art. This repetition of " Portrait of General Washington " becomes comic, and, in spite of my admiration for the original, I could not help being bored. I pointed out, on more than one occasion, the conspicuous absence of another portrait, which surely ought to be there. I mean that of George III., whose foolish obstinacy had as great a share in bringing about American Independence, as had the patriotism and courage of General Washington.

At Philadelphia I and my wife, who had been my companion throughout my long journey, were most hospitably received by an American friend who had been with us on the Yellowstone excursion. Under his auspices we were introduced to everything worth seeing in the historical city, beginning with Independence Hall, where the Declaration of

Independence was signed on July 4, 1776, and from whose steps it was afterwards publicly read.

The American Congress met here until 1797; here Washington was appointed commander of the American army; here in 1787 he resigned his commission into the hands of Congress; and here, in 1796, he issued his farewell address to the people of the United States when he declined to be re-elected to the Presidential chair for a third term. The old Congressional Chamber has been, so far as possible, kept in its original condition. The chairs in which the signers of the Declaration sat are placed round the apartment, and their portraits adorn the walls. I was told that the original simple, unpretending blue check curtains had, by some means, been recovered and again draped the windows. The Academy of Fine Arts, the Masonic Temple, the City Hall (now nearly completed), a magnificent building, the Girard College, and other objects of interest were shown to me in turn.

Finally we drove to Fairmount Park, which is larger by more than 500 acres than our Richmond Park, and, in fact, is the largest park in the world, (for in this comparison I naturally do not include the Yellowstone National Park) being five miles in length by six in width. The Schuylkill River winds through it between lofty and picturesquely-wooded banks.

I am reminded that it was by the foresight of certain citizens, foremost among whom was Mr. George Childs, that this park was secured to the city of Philadelphia. I had the pleasure of making Mr. Childs' acquaintance, as all Englishmen should who visit the Quaker City. Beginning his career as a shop-boy, he is now the wealthy proprietor of the Philadelphia *Public Ledger*—a journal of world wide reputation. His generosity and hospitality are unsurpassed, and he is one of those men who deserve to have riches, because they administer them so wisely. Not only is he the benefactor of his own land, but he delights to honour English literature here and in the mother country. He has put up at his own expense in Westminster Abbey a stained glass window to the memory of the poets George Herbert and William Cowper. He wished to defray the entire cost of the monument in Kensal Green over the then unmarked grave of Leigh Hunt, but was only allowed to give a liberal donation, and he is the largest subscriber to the fund for the window to be erected to the memory of Thomas Moore. His private office in the *Ledger* building is so crowded with objects of artistic value and interest, many of them gifts from friends, that there seems to be no room for anything more. All his life he has been an accumulator of autographs, and his taste and judgment having served him well, he possesses now a most remarkable collection.

I am nearly at the end of my long gossip, and have only one or two additional incidents to mention before quitting the land which had received me so hospitably.

Several competing companies in New York, for a fixed charge per month, will place an instrument in your house, contained in a miniature iron box, having a small crank on the outside. By means of this you can summon at will a boy messenger in uniform, a policeman, a fireman with an extinguisher, or a fire engine.

Breakfasting one morning with Mr. Rufus Hatch, he volunteered to show me how the thing worked.

"Take out your watch," he said, "and note the time." I did so. He turned the crank, and in about fifty seconds a boy in uniform was in the room, breathless with running. Again Mr. Hatch turned his crank and a policeman appeared almost as quickly as the messenger. I seemed incredulous, and half suggested that the whole business had been arranged before. I was asked to choose what the crank should do next.

"Summon another policeman," I said. In a minute a second policeman was standing in the room.

"Shall I call the fire engine?" said Mr. Hatch. But I thought that too serious a matter, and was satisfied with what I had seen. Most of these companies furnish service all night, and houses are often left untenanted, with no protection but that supplied by the electric wires attached to doors and windows, and so contrived that at the neighbouring office it is known instantaneously, not only that a burglar has entered the house, but in which room he is.

My last evening in New York was passed very agreeably, and formed a brilliant termi-

nation to my American trip. Mr. Whitelaw
Reid, the well known editor of the *New York
Tribune*, gave a dinner, of the choicest kind,
in one of the cosy rooms of the Union League
Club, to about sixteen guests, of whom I had
the good fortune to be one. Two Englishmen
besides myself were there, Lord Rosebery and
Mr. Lucy, the clever contributor to more than
one London paper. Among the Americans
present there was scarcely one who was not
distinguished in some way. To begin with
there was the Hon. W. M. Evarts, head and
chief orator of the American Bar. Then
came the Governor and Ex-Governor of the
state of New York, Mr. Edson (the Mayor of
the City of New York); Mr. Hugh J. Jewett
(President of the Erie Railroad); Mr. D. O.
Mills, of California, one of the wealthiest men
in the world—whose daughter is married to
Mr. Whitelaw Reid,—Mr. Joseph Choate, Mr.
Morris K. Jessup, Mr. Chauncey M. Depew,
Mr. Randolph Robinson, Mr. Gresham (the
Postmaster-General); General Bristow, who
was Secretary to the Treasury under General
Grant's Administration; and last, but not
least, Mr. Walter Phelps, Member of Congress

for New Jersey, and formerly American Minister at Vienna. I was assured that there were no less than three of those round the table who were mentioned as probable Presidents of the United States. I shall watch the future with some interest.

Here ends my long story, and I have only to record with a sad pleasure the genial parting from my American host, " Uncle Rufus," who, with many other friends, came to the landing-stage and wished us God-speed as the *Britannic* turned her bows down the Hudson, and so eastward to England.

THE END.

T. VICKERS WOOD, PRINTER, CHURTON ST., S.W.

www.ingramcontent.com/pod-product-compliance
Lightning Source LLC
Chambersburg PA
CBHW022018220426
43663CB00007B/1125